The Aplomb Society

The Aplomb Society

The New Independent Party

DOUGLAS S. HAM

Writers Club Press
San Jose New York Lincoln Shanghai

The Aplomb Society
The New Independent Party

Writers Club Press
an imprint of iUniverse, Inc.

For information address:
iUniverse, Inc.
5220 S. 16th St., Suite 200
Lincoln, NE 68512
www.iuniverse.com

ISBN: 0-595-21582-3

Printed in the United States of America

CONTENTS

ARCHĒ

This book is dedicated to the formation of a NEW INDEPENDENT PARTY called THE APLOMB SOCIETY and the VOTE and the return of the principles, values and virtues that established the Republic of the United States by the Founding Fathers and the thirteen original United Colonies as affirmed by the Declaration of Independence, Articles of Confederation, The Constitution of the United States, Bill of Rights, and Pledge of Allegiance.

This book has been written out of frustration of the downward spiral of integrity the United States has taken in the past forty years. This book expresses my personal opinions and beliefs. It is my sincere hope that the Silent Majority and the Stand-up Citizens make this motif a guide to reestablish the greatness of the United States; to reverse the downward spiral of citizens' non-participation; and to take charge of their rights to be stalwart persons. Becoming aware of and understanding the elements that have caused the deterioration of the fabric of the Republic for the past forty years can only accomplish this, which is one aim of this book. *Nine leading topics*, which have engaged the citizenship from the 1960's to the present day, will be presented and discussed throughout this book.

And I want to give a special thanks to Suzanne Ham and Tommy Harper in their abilities to edit and improve this manuscript.

Douglas S. Ham

December 2001

INTRODUCTION

The federal government has become too large, cumbersome, and ineffective because of bureaucrats' and politicos' ("P-tics") inefficiency based on power greed and arrogance toward the citizens. This inefficiency must not be allowed to continue in the patterns it now operates under. The respect that the United States citizenship has built with other countries in the earlier years has deteriorated to an all time low and is continuing to fall at an alarming rate. This default started in the 1960's when the Majority became silent and the Stand-up Citizens sat down and permitted the immaturity of children to dictate the new liberal rules and agendas as the way of the future. Well, the liberals have had forty years and look at the mess the citizenship and the United States are in today. It is now time for *the citizen VOTE to return* and educate the liberal mentality by introducing what maturity of the mind represents.

The purpose of this book is to (1) demonstrate the total importance of the VOTE, (2) establish a NEW POLITICAL PARTY that will be formed by citizens that register as INDEPENDENT who are centrist thinking voters in all 50 states, (3) give the citizenship a holistic understanding as to the *nine major reasons* why the United States deteriorated to the sorry, passive vulnerable position we now find ourselves, (4) recommend guidelines and the mechanics for establishing and organizing Community-meetings and updating Town-meetings, (5) recommend guideline solutions to help re-establish the path of common sense correctness that God wants us to live by as a

God-respecting nation and as The Founding Fathers debated and then established the foundation of this Republic.

It is now time to return the Republic to the citizenship and its proper place of leadership in the arena of world affairs. Let me introduce you to the vehicle that will accomplish this task. It is called *THE APLOMB SOCIETY*. The Aplomb Society is a NEW POLITICAL PARTY and is being organized, as an *INDEPENDENT PARTY* not aligned with any other party's self-serving doctrine. REGISTERED INDEPENDENT CENTRIST THINKING VOTERS will organize the Aplomb Society through the process of COMMUNITY-MEETINGS and TOWN-MEETINGS, church sponsored meetings, social gatherings, and backyard barbecues in all 50 states. The foundation doctrine for the Aplomb Society is the coming together of the citizenship of each community to present problems that confront the citizens, express opinions, discuss the opinions, vote on the opinions, develop strategies and implement the strategies to solve the problems in established monthly meetings. The prevailing emphasis is to incite people to think—then to action. All Community-meetings and Town-meetings assemblages are open forum only and can be called by any citizen when a subject needs to be presented or a problem is in the way of a citizen's right or a community's or a town's need, as a right given by The Constitution of the United States. The boundaries of a community and a town are given in the EXPOSURE chapter.

Eventually there will be individuals that will emerge as lead representatives of the Aplomb Society. Then, when the first national convention is called, the first leadership will be established. *But first*, the Aplomb Society members must register the Aplomb Society as an Independent Party in each state and then start a concentrated endeavor to elect Independent Registered citizens to the local, county, state and federal offices to establish a solid base in each of the 50 states. There should not be any paid personnel in any position in the Aplomb Society, all positions must be on a volunteer bases.

THE APLOMB SOCIETY is not being organized to change or rewrite the Constitution. *THE APLOMB SOCIETY* is being organized to reestablish the Constitution as the guideline to proper governing of a free society by bringing the citizens back to the understanding that they are the administrators of their destiny, not the P-tics, judges, bureaucrats, or liberals with personal agendas who feed out of the public tax trough. The Founding Fathers agreed to and derived the powers to form Our Republic from the consent of the voting citizens of the original 13 States for the protection and benefit of the people. And, we must return to that mandate. The following important Motifs will bring back to remembrance the importance of the individual VOTE as a catalyst to needed changes.

This MOTIF *is about the power of the* VOTE and what we have forgotten or overlooked. The VOTE has two truisms: (1) The *VOTE* is the single most powerful voice that exists; and (2) The *VOTE* is the single loudest voice that exists. The necessity is to remember why this Republic was founded and to recapture the concepts of understanding of the values and virtues of the 10 Commandments, Ordinances and Statutes of God, the desires of the Founding Fathers and the original 13 States, the ability to meet as neighbors in viable active open Community-meetings or Town-meetings to discuss items of importance, and about the citizens of the Republic having a moral obligation to help bring every *legitimate* citizen of the Republic into the mainstream of opportunity.

We are an interwoven single nation of diverse cultures that claims one allegiance to one Republic of the United States in which we live, not a fractured nation made up of islands of separatism based on a hyphen(-) to divide the American citizenship into liberal play-offs as is the perception today. The need is to stand-up to the twaddle of the liberal activism of judges, the liberal despotisms of government, the liberal left media, the conservative right media and the truism that some individuals are always "filled with a passion for inequality" as Aristotle stated. Most likely his opinion was based on tyranny's duel foundation of childish paranoia and self-elevation due to intolerance of others' ideas, opinions, or positions. This immaturity must be eliminated at once.

This MOTIF is *not about a debate* on slavery reparation, political correctness, affirmative action, civil rights, women's lib or any other special interest grabs. It is about the *voting right* and *obligation* the United States citizen has to themselves, their families, and the Republic in which they live.

"When you become entitled to exercise the right of voting for public offices, let it be impressed on your mind that God commands you to choose for rulers just men who will rule in the fear of God. The preservation of a republican government depends on the faithful discharge of this duty: if the citizens neglect their duty and place unprincipled men in office, the government will soon be corrupted." *Noah Webster (1758–1843).*

It is time to stand up, citizens, and take this country back from the personal interest judicial judges, left liberals, P-tics, bureaucrats, left media and the far conservative right media by reestablishing the Republic as the Constitution states and the Founding Fathers signed. The Constitution is the glue for the Republic as the Mother is the glue that causes a family to function as a unit.

EXPOSURE

To refresh our understanding as to why and how our Republic came into existence, we need to start by recalling the major reasons the original pilgrims boarded ships and came to the shores of Plymouth in 1620. The primary elements that caused the mass exodus from England were the picayune arrogance of the King, his friends and the business elitist, the injustice endured from the justice system and religious despotism, the lack of personal rights, and the cleaning out of prisons, to name a few. This was more than enough to cause people to seek out a haven in which to establish freedom from tyranny.

With this mass exodus, the pilgrims brought with them the *spirit of independence* of self-worth, religious freedom to worship God as their foundation and the 10 Commandments as the root and path to salvation. The pilgrims came to set their own destiny through the right of free choice by the vote, land ownership, economic self-sufficiency and to establish a government for the benefit of the citizens, not for the benefit of self-serving P-tics, judges, bureaucrats and special interest parasites.

Even before the pilgrims landed in 1620 at Plymouth Rock, the process had already started in the early 1500's when traders and explorers started arriving in search of new opportunities. In 1585 England tried to establish the Roanoke colony and a second attempt was made in 1587. It took the 13 colonies a span of 125 years to organize a government of the people, starting with the formation of the Virginia colony of Jamestown in April of 1607 until the Georgia colony was formed at Savannah in 1732. Before the founding of the government, the colonies alliance was based on cooperation and not on a unified agreement of one flag and one constitution. The complex work of establishing the future United States started in earnest in Philadelphia on May 10, 1775 with the convening of the Second Continental Congress. This Congress became the nation's first national government serving as such from July 4, 1776, at the adoption of the Declaration of Independence, until March 1, 1781 when the Articles of Confederation became effective. Then came The Constitution of the United States, ratified on March 17, 1787, and the Bill of Rights, ratified December 15, 1791.

If you read the Declaration of Independence carefully and with passion, you will discover the heart and soul of the Republic of the United States' reason for existing:

"*Resolved*, That these United Colonies are, and of right ought to be, free and independent States, that they are absolved from all allegiance to the British Crown, and that all political connection between them and the State of Great Britain is, and ought to be, totally dissolved." (July 2, 1776)

"When in the Course of human events, it becomes necessary for one people to dissolve the political bands which have connected them with another, and to assume among the powers of the earth, the separate and equal station to which the Laws of nature and of Nature's God entitle them, a decent respect to the opinions of mankind requires that they should declare the cause which impel them to the separation."

"We hold these truths to be self-evident, that all men are created equal, that they are endowed by their Creator with certain unalienable Rights, that among these are Life, Liberty and the pursuit of Happiness. That to secure these rights, Governments are instituted among Men, deriving their just powers from the consent of the governed; that whenever any Form of Government becomes destructive of these ends it is the Right of the People to alter or to abolish it, and to institute new Government, laying its foundations on such principles and organizing its power in such form, as to them shall seem most likely to effect their Safety and Happiness. Prudence, indeed, will dictate that Governments long established should not be changed for light and transient causes; and accordingly all experience shown, that mankind are more disposed to suffer, while evils are sufferable, than to right themselves by abolishing the forms to which they are accustomed. But when a long train of abuses and usurpations, pursuing invariably the same Objects evinces a design to reduce them under absolute Despotism, it is their right, it is their duty, to throw off such Government, and to provide new Guards for their future security,"

"And for the support of this Declaration, with a firm reliance on the protection of Divine Providence, we mutually pledge to each other, our lives, our Fortunes, and our sacred Honor." (July 4, 1776-*Extracted*)

What is unique about the Declaration of Independence is that it exudes the *spirit of independence* the pilgrims brought with them. The "Spirit" took rise on May 10, 1775—like a great Phoenix Bird—when the Founding Fathers said *enough is enough* and threw the British Crown out of controlling their rights and destiny. This "Spirit" of taking charge of their rights and their destiny is our inheritance from the 13 original United Colonies. But, the one guiding concept they clearly understood and established as the cornerstone at the inception was *that God must be the Spiritual Leader of the Republic* if the United States was destined to become a mature nation and a true world leader.

What the "Spirit" will do for the citizenship is force the return to a Republic as the Founding Fathers set up and eliminate the oligarchic restricted left liberal democratic entrenchment that has developed over the past 40 years. The silent majority citizens must now—*this day*—stand-up and shout *'that is enough'*. Then they must start organizing citizens' Community/Town meetings to bring the citizenship together, develop agendas of topics to be discussed, develop strategies, vote on changes in the VOTING booth and stand up to the liberal judicial activism. And, the first order of citizen business is to RECALL the entrenched P-tics, political judges and bureaucrats, THEN REPLACE them with citizens of proven common sense that are not connected with special interest groups or have their own agenda. Their agenda must be the citizenship's agenda.

What the Founding Fathers *did not want* was a strong central government that had total authority and control over the citizens of the Republic. Control over the citizenship is the scenario the left liberal Democratic Party and cohorts want and they have been trying to manipulate the citizenship for the past 40 years into a P-tic autocratic characteristic society. The so-called public policies they have pushed through are almost endless on any subject you care to name. But, what is so sad is that the silent 75% majority citizenry is to be held equally responsible for becoming complacent and self-destructive by giving decision making responsibilities and their vote to the 10% left liberal democratic party's fragmented coalition to establish its rules for governing and controlling the citizenship. Does this point to the silent citizenship as leader/owner of their constitutional rights or wagging tail of the liberal arrogance? Fortunately, there is always 15% of the citizenship that fights to retain a check and balance system against takeover endeavors and protects the rights granted to the citizenship by the Constitution. *Stand Up Citizens*, reestablish the Republic and reclaim your right to decide your direction in life by taking your VOTE back from political hacks, incompetent judges and left liberals. Let's put the governing of the Citizens of the Republic in correct order for the joy and benefit of the Citizenship.

The majority citizenship has become a non-participant by leaving it to others to speak in their stead. This permits the 10% take over rule. If the time is taken to verify this fact, you will discover that every country that has permitted a left wing element to come to power has this 10% behind them when they start taking over the government executive branch, the judicial departments and the military. Fortunately, our military leaders and soldiers have loyal integrity to the citizenship and the Republic.

Then the left wing element starts infiltrating other governmental departments, committees, and commissions by replacing the bureaucrats and staffs with their fellow travelers. This tactic is how the slapstick of *the fellow travelers society* begins to entrench themselves and start their control over the citizenship because of *citizen non-participation*. This situation now exists in the United States because you—silent majority—have become so engrossed in your existence, you gave the 10% fellow travelers the free hand to vote for you and tell you how you are to live under their rules.

The managing of the Republic is so messed up it makes you want to kick something. Understand this, the liberal left is trying to twist the Republic into a left wing democracy and they are doing it *by voting for you* when *you do not show up to vote*. Listen to this grandmothers, grandfathers, mothers, fathers, daughters, and sons—*all of you who do not VOTE*, even in the smallest voting event, you have given up your responsibility to control your or your family's destination by turning your responsibilities over to the liberal despots.

What is your vision of the Republic as it is controlled today? Are you happy with that vision? How do you get rid of this twisted self-styled democracy that the liberal Democratic Party and left media have been entrenching for the past 40 years? Think about this, 100%—10% = 90% that has the power to *shine the light* on the liberal left Democratic Party and the left media. Your vision is yours. To get rid of the political thorn is to pull it out with a VOTE and elect common sense citizens to office. To get rid of the left oriented media is to turn them off.

Why do we—the citizens—always ask, "Why doesn't the government do something to fix a problem"? Do you mean, fix a problem they have put into play? What a joke that is. My question to you is—why don't you, as voting citizens, call the citizens of your community and town together in a collective meeting and solve the problem yourselves? That is how our ancestors took care of serious business. Why do or would you want a liberal, bureaucrat, P-tic, or judge to set up their rules and guidelines for you to follow? All you are doing is turning your destiny over to them. The happenings in Florida are premiere examples of self-serving lawyers, entrenched P-tics and political judges telling you what you will accept or not accept, whether you like it or not.

Representatives are elected to serve the will of the voters who voted them into their positions, not to establish a home for themselves by selling votes to special interest greed and then trying to persuade the voters back home that they did the right thing by just keeping quiet as to what they have done. Citizens, make your elected P-tics justify, in an open Community/Town meeting, their election to office by requiring them to explain each vote they cast and who it benefited. And, *ASK* who are they serving, special interest greed or the voters. Also, tell them to explain, by line item, where the money comes from that they receive and why they received it.

Keep in mind that *a full time* P-tic, judge or bureaucrat living a political life is nothing more than an opportunity for them to live off other people's labor and feed out of the public's tax trough. P-tics "act in their own economic self-interest, as well as the perceived self-interest of their constituents". The P-tic life "is so rigged to protect incumbents that it amounts to a monopoly" and has lead to the abuse and misuse of the federal government structure for the sake of establishing personal power greed. And, it is a well-known fact that P-tics always legislates too much to try to justify their election.

It is now time to spread the knowledge of government management around by *setting term limits* for judges, P-tics, and agency directors. Setting term limits would create a growing CITIZENS' MANAGEMENT TRAINING ARENA that would develop: working knowledge of legislative procedures, executive experience and knowledge in how to manage the Republic for the benefit of the citizens', economic growth, job provision, bringing business owners and citizens together, protecting the environment from the environmentalist and self-serving corporations, and maintaining the security of the United States from outside and inside forces.

One of the Slick-Willie ways Washington P-tics, agency bureaucrats and judges by-pass the citizen vote and stick it to the citizenship and business owners is to set their rules and guidelines as if their rules and guidelines are the law of the land and the bureaucrats and judges are the administrators of the new law. The one thing you should understand is that if they get away with it long enough, that verbiage will become "assumed" to be the law. Whenever an agency issues new rules or guidelines, challenge those rules in *a friendly court of common sense* and make the bureaucrats put all their contacts and deals, which they made with others, on the table. Also be aware that a lot of P-tics hide behind this process so they will not have to publicly display the way they personally believe or vote on the subject. There are Senate rules that allow members to oppose legislation without going public. I guess this is the cowards' way out for them.

Let's reform your mind-set, resurrect and replant the "seedbed" of correct values, virtues, free speech without stupidity, and come to conclusions with common sense reality. Always keep in mind that liberal ideology is the perversion of wisdom. You have the Constitutional right and obligation to raise your voice in opposition to liberal rhetoric stew, grandiloquence, bombast or shuck and jive you find offensive. *Stand Up Citizen*! Let YOUR VOTING VOICE be heard!

The war to recapture the essence of the spirit of the original 13 States and take the Republic back from Judical activism, left liberals, bureaucrats and P-tics will only be accomplished by the esprit put forth in neutralizing the liberal left mentality by establishing the Community/Town agendas as the only agenda. To do this will require an understanding of organization, tactics, and boundaries of issues. This will also require the ability to recognize the methodologies used by the *fellow travelers* on the left liberal side when you attend a meeting. The liberal facades will be covered in depth in the EMPTINESS chapter of this book.

To start the process, I ask you to reread the Introduction to refresh your memory as to the purpose of *THE APLOMB SOCIETY*. There is an urgent need to organize in each Community/Town, as the Republican and Democratic conventions so vividly pointed out with their massive shopping lists of useless and pork barrel waste of things they will force upon the taxpaying citizens. The Republican side was for all the people but overseen by federal legislations and to be administered mostly by state bureaucrats. The Democrat side was for the low and lower middle income people but controlled by federal P-tic legislation, to be administered by federal bureaucrats and special interest groups and add "200" new federal programs. The reasons for establishing A TOTALLY NEW REGISTERED INDEPENDENT CENTRIST

POLITICAL PARTY, organized through the open alliance community movement will be projected throughout the book.

Forget the wounds of history; they are as obsolete as a sphinx. *Get over it, Get past it,* and *Get on with it (life)*. Approach the situation for what it is, and nothing more; whether you like it or not is irrelevant. No matter which stand you take, do not think of it as a position; think only of it as a beginning process to a solution. Take the most effective stance according to the circumstances. The throes of a long overdue restructuring of the Republic is in the minds of the non-self-serving voting citizenship now more than ever before and must be done from the INDEPENDENT CENTER POSITION. *Stand-up citizens*—call the Community/Town together and find out what people are thinking. Always remember, the only kind of thinking that will hold up under careful examination is logical thinking—thinking that is reasonable, reliable, and believable—above all.

The most productive path to your rightful place in line at the voting booth is the open forum Community/Town meeting assemblage. (A COMMUNITY'S BOUNDARY is the furthest homestead property in any direction from the Courthouse of the closest city/town with which the homestead family transacts business. This circle is called the S.M.S.A. (standard metropolitan statistical area)). In larger cities the S.M.S.A. area becomes confusing, so I would use what the local neighborhood residences call the Community. (Remember, TOWN-MEETINGS are contained by the boundaries of the city/town proper).

The one firm rule that will make a meeting successful is that everyone has equal time to present his or her topics of concern to the citizenship by the process of "freedom of critique". Setting up the physical mechanics of a meeting can be handled by anyone with the knowledge. The elements for organizing meetings follow in the next paragraph. *But remember*, participation in a Community/Town meeting requires maturity of patience and respect to each participant. To support the right to be a stalwart person and a United States citizen under the Constitution of the Republic, you must be willing to stand up for and protect any legitimate citizen's right to state his/her view or to oppose a view of others on any subject no matter how opposite it is to your point of view, as long as the subject is on correct legitimate ground and is not immoral in content. If the content is not applicable, just pass it by and go on to a germane subject. The foundation of a Community-meeting or a Town-meeting is the coming together of like thinking citizens who meet to express opinions, discuss the opinions, vote on the opinions, develop strategy, and implement the strategy for the betterment of the citizenship. When there is a problem confronting the citizens such as removing a P-tic, a judge or a bureaucrat from office, placing an initiative on a ballot or confronting the city council or county officials, call the citizens to a Community/Town meeting.

There are ELEMENTS connected with open meetings you must become aware of as follows.

First, you will find very concerned people wanting to discuss the issues in an open forum.

Second, you will encounter the left liberal media when they start a media blitz through their "raree-shows" conducted by the clichés and sound bites of no substance pundits, pensters and weasel wordsmiths to establish their positions.

Third, you will be confronted with left of center liberals, the left media and the P-tics that show up at a meeting because their agenda is prejudiced against your point of view. Left liberals have different tactics to try to control a meeting through disruption or derailing the agenda by making every attempt to push their agenda and keep the people from participating. You will quickly become aware of their attempts to suppress opposition, to show disrespect toward anyone who opposes them or intolerance to anyone who wants to speak, and to keep the citizenship uninformed. Unfortunately, this low mentality has spread to the smallest communities.

Fourth, there are two types of *outside the political mainstream* political people: (1) a person who does not have the knowledge of a subject being presented or the self-confidence to express themselves out loud. There by opening the door of acceptance so he/she can easily be twisted to follow someone else's prepackaged easy to sallow rhetoric philosophy; and (2) a venal *gadfly doing their buck and wing gadfly bovine plop* (as defined in the Emptiness chapter) harangue speech and raree-show. This type has a consuming ambition to pole vault into the ranks of the power elite by trying to organize philistine bovine mentalities to back their self-centered plan to infiltrate the ranks of the ruling elite or at second best to bluff their way into the second echelon of P-tic decision-making *or* trying to get someone to pay them to front their cause. Always ask who sent them and who is paying them to cause trouble. Find this answer and use it against the opposition. What is so pathetic is that the gadfly does not understand the other side of the coin. And, that is that the power elite will use the gadfly to hide behind to stay out of the public's eye while they carry out their agenda. This mockery of seriousness tricks the gadfly into a false impression that they have power. The only perceived power they acquire is the power handed out to them by their own kind of self-serving parasites. It is called *'pea pod power'*.

The left media, newsprint and wire, have become antiquated dinosaurs that would not know substance if it bit them on their dingus. The liberal intelligence is different because they have less reasoning ability than others and that their thinking ability is verified by their writing in clichés, sound bites and lack of substance. *But*, if you do locate an in-the-middle newsperson that, (1) has no ego to see their name on a by-line, (2) understands the definition of common sense truth writing, (3) does not espouse to either side of a viewpoint and (4) knows how to listen without interruption, that is a person with whom to talk. This type of newsperson is explained in the Media section.

Fifth, to be able to control your Community/Town meeting you must be able to recognize liberal methodology. You need to be aware of liberal traits, presentations or tactics that they bring to a meeting. Once you recognize a scenario, you can cut them off at the knees by taking charge of the agenda and topics being discussed. The Emptiness chapter of the book will give you a holistic understanding of how liberals operate. But, for you to be able to take charge of a meeting, become well aware of the following liberal "paranoid position" tactic that they used to gain access into meetings.

To control a meeting or subject they oppose, they will try flooding a meeting with conspiracy advocates. These are different groups, all with high-sounding names thrown out for fake intimidation, colored by fear or exaggeration for political effect. Almost all of these liberal clumps only have one or two members. The only reason they try this bullyrag is that they have gotten away with it before because of the lack of knowledge of the citizens they browbeat. For you to eliminate this nonsense just close the meeting to outsiders at the door and *only admit* the Community/Town citizenship by checking addresses from drivers' licenses.

This effort will not eliminate all left liberals, as there might be some that live in the Community/Town and they should be admitted. But, watch out for a guest they try to slip into the meeting. Make it known at the beginning of the meeting that everyone is to speak as individual citizens and not as being a representative of some group or a P-tic office. If an outsider does infiltrate the meeting and tries to sneak in their affiliation or tries to get the floor, stop the sneak attack and tell them to leave. If they refuse to leave have them removed by the appointed sergeant at arms or call the police and make sure the citizens back the police up. At the door, you need to have one or two strong willed intellectual checkers to encounter the shock of rejection because to a liberal it is outrageous to be prevented from doing whatever they wish. The liberal elements will then try to force their way back in by any means, even threatening to sue. This threat is nothing more than a small mind spewing out arrogance. A liberal will sink to any depth to get their way.

If you do invite a newsperson, be sure, by reading their articles, that they are not a liberal reporter. Make sure they are of the caliber noted in the previous paragraph. Understand that the meeting was called for the Community/Town citizenship, not for outsiders. Since the meeting is by invitation, it is no different than inviting someone over to your house, it just happens to be a bigger house.

You now know how to call a Community/Town meeting and what to be aware of in setting up a meeting. The fun part is the camaraderie that will develop in bringing the Community/Town together by working for the same community security. Never give your vote away again. *After the community has voted on an issue to be addressed*, there will be *the need to set up* FOUR SEPARATE UNCONNECTED GROUPS *to bring the issue to a proper conclusion*. What is meant by unconnected is that each group will have their own separate agenda to accomplish with their own deadlines. All will come together in the end. Never permit any type of judge, P-tic, bureaucrat, left liberal reporter or left liberal to be on any of these committees. The groups are as follows and will work closely with each other:

(1) *Intelligence gathering and Analyses Group(IAG)*—the responsibility will be to analyze the issue and decide what information will need to be collected. After all data has been collected and put into correct order, the package will be turned over to the Planning Group. Also locate who the opposition is and build a file on them. Intelligence gathering will be an ongoing process year-round. Files and subject concerns need a continuing update.

(2) *Planning Group(PG)*—the group responsibilities will be to organize the information received from the IAG and develop a plan for presentation to the community. When the plan is finished, the group will call a Community/Town meeting to present the plan for discussion and hold a vote for implementation or rejection of the plan. Remember, majority rules, but always add into the minutes of the meeting a proviso that the minority position is noted along with the majority position. If the plan develops a snag and after an evaluation for the reason the snag developed, go over the minority position and see if a different merge method can be incorporated to make the plan work. Then resubmit the plan for discussion and a vote to the Community/Town members. This group will also be

responsible for developing the *Voter-crafted Initiatives* as explained in the section labeled Voter-crafted Initiatives.

(3) *Advertising Assault Group(AAG)*—This group will have three agendas. The *first* is to keep the Community/Town abreast of plan development and problems to be solved. The group will ask the community for help when information is needed by the Planning Group or any other group. There are citizens that can obtain information that the group my not be able to get. *Second*, is to develop counter-hostile perceptions through a no-holds-barred advertising assault when the liberals and the left media start their attack on the community's decision concerning an issue. Always be ready for the left media blitz attack. *Third*, the group will also be responsible for helping the Planning Group to develop the Voter-crafted Initiatives as explained in the section labeled *Voter-crafted Initiatives* and placing them on the ballot to be voted on.

(4) *Events Group(EG)*—The responsibility is to notify the Community/Town of all meetings and events. They are to help the Advertising Assault Group, when requested, to get the word out when time is of the essence. They are also to set up the elements for physical meetings, select the sergeant at arms and the checkers at the door.

The following are a few additional observations you need to be aware of to achieve a successful Community/Town meeting:

(1) Frame issues for the maximum appeal.

(2) Present the citizens with issues that have substance. The citizens need to get their teeth of understanding into the issue to cause action to take place.

(3) Caucasian voters have begun to assume the political habits of a minority. They are developing protective instincts like minority groups do. This does nothing but create islands of separatism that demonstrate distrust of self and of others and greed. Everyone needs to put a stop to this kind of thinking. Separatism just creates useless prejudices that pit citizens against each other.

(4) The greater percentage of citizens feels small in the scheme of things around them. This means they have not found their position in which to excel. It is time to get the entire community involved. Ask each person how he or she wants to become involved and help him or her to become involved.

(5) Simplicity is the key to success in solving an issue. Don't clutter with psychological barriers.

(6) Social reality—the words "social", "political correctness" and "affirmative action" are nothing more than made up liberal words to box someone in or a concept to inhibit the growth of an idea for the control or benefit of a single person or a selected group of individuals.

(7) "Social Order" is a phrase that does not mean much because there are too many variables.

(8) Leadership is what is needed now—not the liberal left verbiage that is espoused and entrenched with corruption of the truth.

(9) The liberals will go to any length to build a consensus.

(10) Ask citizens for their active participation in the reshaping of the Republic.

(11) Always point out disinformation that anyone starts putting out to the public. You will be surprised how gullibly the public latches onto

completely unsubstantiated gossip. Liberals provide disinformation and then play on the hysteria generated by the disinformation.

(12) Simply forcing an issue out into the open is enough to begin the process of dialogue.

(13) To be maligned by the left media cucarachas is a badge of pride and another hole in their babble.

These are thirteen major points that each person should keep in mind as rules of engagement in developing THE APLOMB SOCIETY Community/Town meetings and to prevent being caught unaware by a situation.

Let us now look at *FIVE DIFFERENT MAJOR PROBLEMS* that will affect a Community/Town from *the outside.* As you know, there are many sub-topics that will or will not affect a community and are germane only to a particular community or region. The following are subjects connected to all communities. If a concern does surface, get the community involved at once by calling a Community/Town meeting as outlined previously. The five subjects of discussion that follow are *POLLS, VOTER-CRAFTED INITIATIVES, THE JUSTICE SYSTEM, ILLEGAL ALIENS AND THE MEDIA.*

We will start with the POLL by defining what a poll is supposed to represent. The true reason to commission a poll is to find out what public opinion is on a subject. The majority of polls are used to justify a position or sway public opinion. A poll should be about truth; but it is designed to manipulate. Unfortunately, the gullibility of the public is to believe whatever a poll twist comes up with and the media disseminates as the truth. This mindset must be eradicated. What is so sad about this mindset is that most of the time the public gives up their right and obligation to themselves to find out the truth about what is being told to them. The only true poll is the final count of the citizens' votes at the ballot box.

There are legitimate reasons to commission a poll. But, the Presidential election of 2000 demonstrated the total uselessness of public polls and illustrates that they no longer serve a legitimate political purpose. Sadly, the majority of polls have evolved from legitimacy into the twisting of the truth for personal greed. The results that are created by the pensters and weasel wordsmiths have branded them with lack labels of: (a) loss of integrity, and (b) a person of no substance. Labels causing their families embarrassment and the sponsors of the poll who employ them with the same two labels.

Let's examine the shameless shuck and jive pandering that goes into most polls. *There are three types of polls.* (1) The first poll is called the honest poll and is taken at local meetings. This type of poll will reflect the audience's belief on a subject before or after discussion of a subject of local concern, then is voted on by a show of hands or by ballot; (2) Next there are two types of pandering poll twisting scenarios with which you are inundated from the "news mongers" that saturate the public like a pond full of polliwogs. They are as follows.

Now let's look at *the first kind of twisting* and *the compositions* that make up this type of poll and what drives them:

(a) Left liberals, far right conservatives, the left liberal media, the right conservative media, P-tics, and special interest lobbying artists cite this type of poll result as if they are the authority;

(b) The questions put into this poll are worded as the sponsor wants so that the results will favor their position;

(c) The sponsors' spin-doctors espouse this poll as if it trumps the issues of truth or law;

(d) Instant polls are being used to justify almost any position for next day influence;

(e) Sponsors of a poll use polls to alter or entrench a position for their benefit;

(f) The public becomes confused because of the diversity of so many polls on the same subject;

(g) If the citizens are not knowledgeable of the issue that the poll is addressing, it could cause a false inflation of the influence of a sponsor;

(h) Most polls are taken by spin-doctors to measure the emotional reaction to what someone has said or done so it can be used against them;

(i) Spin-doctors use polls to fuzzy issues when their sponsor or the political party they are associated with is in trouble and the truth needs to be hidden.

The second type of twisting poll is the scurvy of all polls and is called a "push poll" which is a sham survey designed to slur a candidate. It is driven by false information based on the misleading, untrue, or deceptive innuendos. And, you became well aware of this type of "push poll" used extensively in the Presidential election of 2000 by the political sophism mongers. When you discover this type of poll being used, make it a priority to expose the author and defeat the person or the subject it will benefit.

Question for the parents. Do you permit your children to use in your relationship the kind of verbiage the spin-doctor and weasel wordsmiths types do? Of course not! If you do not accept that sleaze from your children, why would you lower the family standards in front of the children by participating in a poll that will shuck and jive the truth associated with smear campaigns worded with truth twisting disinformation? You should sit down with the family and teach them how the authors of such nonsense write truth twisting. Then, each family member should be assigned an area of research to find out the truth the author is trying to hide. Next, sit down as a family and have each member present his findings. Now, take a family vote as to how the family wants to vote on the issue and then the parents vote that way. Not only does this process teach the children to do research, it also teaches them how to make correct decisions when they are confronted with daily elements of life when there is no one around to help them.

VOTER-CRAFTED INITIATIVES are the delight of a sponsor who spends the time and money to qualify an initiative to be placed on a ballot and have it passed by the voters. The initiative is also the ratatouille of the weasel wordsmith in most cases. There is a third element to the initiative process and that is a political judge who slides with the political or liberal wind. He/she makes the decision whether or not the citizenship will be allowed their constitutional right to vote on an initiative. The opposition to the initiative originates the decision process of denial or approval to let the citizenship vote.

It is a citizen's responsibility to become knowledgeable about the correct construction of an initiative to eliminate the judicial denial. There are some very simple steps of which you must become aware as follows:

(1) To qualify an initiative, a sponsor must know the laws and rules for the construction of properly wording the initiative. Also, take it to an initiative knowledgeable attorney to help with the legalities needed *and* make sure he/she knows the time tables for filing any memorandums required to back up the initiative;

(2) Always pick up the official petitions from the right government department and make sure you have more than enough copies;

(3) Know who can legally sign the initiative and the number of signatures needed to be able to turn the petition into the correct voter signature validation-counting department;

(4) Always make doubly sure you have at least twenty-five percent more names than you need to qualify;

(5) There can be only one issue per initiative and the wording must be factually stated and not misleading. There cannot be two or more separate issues on one voter-crafted initiative at the same time;

(6) Make sure the initiative is submitted in a way that will allow the citizen to understand that the issue in the initiative is a single issue only;

(7) Make absolutely sure you turn in all the initiative documents at one time to the correct government offices as far in advance as possible so as to eliminate any time constraints because of challenges;

(8) Have your initiative attorney lined up so he/she can attack any challenges or irregularities immediately; and

(9) Always research who is leading the charge against your initiative. To know the enemy is to defeat him!

There is one additional element you will come up against besides the liberals and the judicial wind. That is the voter elected P-tic that administers a publicly funded bureaucratic state, city, or federal agency and takes sides publicly on a citizen-crafted initiative. It is irregular and totally out of line with all political walls of separation between the voting citizenship and the bureaucratic work force paid for by the taxes the citizenship sends to the different government entities. This type of P-tic should be subject to an immediate recall vote from office by the citizenship.

THE JUSTICE SYSTEM is continually pointing up the dark underside of abstract liberal laws, radical patterns of paranoia, judicial activism and self-serving greed that demonstrate the void of correct common sense and flaunt the moral turpitude of legal judgments.

Have you become aware that court judges are disfranchising or nullifying your votes for passage of desired citizens' issues more and more each year? This looks to be in direct violation of Amendment 15, Section 1 of the Constitution. All these disfranchising decisions must be challenged each time they are published. Also, the need to take the courts back from judicial liberalism stems from another fact that more and more judges are espousing judicial activism in support of one-sided civil rights, protection of criminals, other idiosyncrasies of favoritism toward the sleaze establishments, and of liberal hypocrisy. It looks like the liberals and liberal judges are trying to micro manage your destiny and trying to turn your beliefs to mirror the liberal scenarios.

Because of the subversion of runaway court judges, the judicial courts' credibility is in a major deterioration dive. They have clearly overstepped the authority given in the Constitution because of their presumption of judicial prerogative. Decisions by the judicial activism of courts are telling the citizenship that their majority vote does not count because informal political decisions made by P-tics, special "hands extended" interest groups and liberal arrogates are overriding what the majority of citizens want to happen.

Because the overrides are becoming commonplace, a prevailing public belief has emerged that the P-tics, bureaucrats, and judges have become so complacent and cocksure of permanent longevity that they are telling the citizens to shut-up and do as they are told. It is strongly suggested that these liberal divas read for the first time or reread the Declaration of Independence. After the reading, they should become totally aware that there is a new push to clean out the divas that ignore the rights of the voting citizenship. And, a common agenda to replace the source of the immoral decisions being forced upon the citizens is being discussed more and more throughout the Republic and is being acted upon at the voting booth.

Due to the number of federal and state judges flaunting their contempt for the majority's will of the Republic's citizenship, it is now time for all citizens to become knowledgeable of the processes involved *in impeachment* and *stand for recall*. Read Article III, Section 1 of the Constitution and you will see it does not guarantee any judge his position for life. It states, "The judges, both of the supreme and inferior courts, shall hold their office during good behavior....". The impeachment process is used whenever a judge attempts to affront the will of the people, introducing arbitrary powers, judicial misconduct, disloyalty, perjury, and disregarding the citizens' interests. Impeachment ensures that the citizenship will not become slaves to un-elected judges.

Left liberal judges and co-horts have demonstrated during the past 40 years their loss of judicial integrity by countering common-sense public policy and acting as the legislative spokesman for the radical left liberal agenda through judicial activism. No appointed or elected judicial person should be so independent that they take it upon themselves to become unaccountable to the Citizenship. It is now time THE APLOMB SOCIETY silent majority and stand-up citizens start organizing Community/Town meetings and start identifying all the left liberal judges, useless P-tics and arrogant bureaucrats for removal from their office. It is time to replace them with citizens of proven integrity and common sense.

The 1st Amendment of the Constitution has been so trampled upon and twisted with liberal arrogance it has become a blur of the original intent. One example is that The 1st Amendment states "Congress shall make no law respecting an establishment of religion, or prohibiting the free exercise thereof, or abridging the freedom of speech, or of the press; or the right of the people peaceably to assemble, and to petition the government for a redress of grievances." That is explicit enough for any person who reads and writes English to understand the definitions taken from any English compiled dictionary on the words: *RELIGION, SPEECH, ASSEMBLY,* and *PETITION*. But, the Supreme Court, State Supreme Courts, and a number of federal and state judges have taken it upon themselves with their perceived authority to twist the definitions of the words SPEECH and RELIGION to the arrogate whims of the weasel word-smiths of liberals, ACLU and trial attorney co-horts.

It is well documented that the judicial system has redefined the word SPEECH to give free "speech interpretation" to anyone espousing sleaze or liberalism on any subject. It is now time to introduce the so-called legal system practitioners to the correct definition of the word "speech" as printed in the unabridged dictionary of English words. The wording of the definition starts with "The faculty or power of speaking; oral communication; ability to express one's thoughts and emotions by speech sounds and gesture". And the definition continues on in depth. Somewhere in the past a judicial weasel wordsmith convinced a like-minded judge to also include picture pornography as free speech out of the mouth. Now that is a stretch by any sense of the imagination—even for a left-liberal judge. This is just another example of twisting the Constitution and trying to legitimatize visual pictures of filth for personal profit. This includes the "sleaze society's" desire to legitimatize unrestricted freedom to approach and have sex with any age child as the American Civil Liberties Union (ACLU) has illustrated by stepping in to defend the North American Man-Boy Love Association (NAMBLA) to have the right to prey on children. Talk about a sick defense. The ACLU is also trying to twist the 1st Amendment to use "freedom of speech" by trying to slide the "freedom of association" rhetoric into the court case as being speech. The big question is—what has "freedom of association" got to do with the 1st Amendment?

Another twist of judicial activism gives a mother and her doctor the right to murder a child when the child is already coming out of the mother's birth canal by cutting the skull of a fetus and draining the brain contents before extracting the body. Is there any difference between birth canal murder and killing the child just as it has cleared the womb? When a fetus is created—it is a beginning human—not a thing to be murdered after developing full term by an irresponsible, unstable person that needs a mental makeup overhaul and greed by sleaze doctors that want a new car or a country club membership. *Again*, giving the criminals their rights over the victims' rights has been a cornerstone of liberal judicial decisions for many, many years just to name a few immoral turpitudes.

The American Civil Liberties Union has taken on the roll of Lucifer's advocate howler for the oppression of the First Amendment protection of free speech against God's Church. It is perceived that the ACLU's contention of belief is that everyone or any perverse group has the right of free speech about any subject, but not the American citizen who wants to express God's religious instructions in public places such as prayer in a classroom or at an athletic event or the use of public school buildings to discuss the biblical scriptures by holding a meeting for their members. The twisted definition espoused by the weasel wordsmiths of the *wall of separation* of Church and State has been a joke from the first and has never had any legitimacy just as the teaching of evolution does not have one fact to establish its legitimacy.

The so-called foundation for the premise for justification of separation of Church and State stems from just two letters. The first letter was written by The Danbury Baptist Association,

October 7, 1801 to President Thomas Jefferson and the second letter was his answer dated January 1, 1802. You are encouraged to read these two letters.

The ambiguousness of President Jefferson's response letter has become the parasitic connection for the liberal spirit of interpretation for the separation of Church and State for the weasel wordsmiths. By permitting liberal religious intolerance, there has evolved the privilege of twisting the legal, political, and historical "will of the majority, the Natural law of every society." Because of this liberal spirit of interpretation gone amok, the religious citizen is having to fight the liberal judical winds of tyranny.

The results of liberal judicial philosophy are that the judicial morality of law decisions in the United States has put the federal and state justice systems in a barrel of slop in the eyes of United States citizens. The twisting of the word RELIGION, by the federal and state court systems, has initiated a drive by the liberal elements to eliminate the learning of morality concepts that is taught by religious doctrine of correct conduct and proper interaction with others in public and private events. The major question each voting citizen should personally ask the liberal judges of the Supreme Court and the other judges is 'why did you make it your business to eliminate from the Constitutional fabric of the Republic the divine guidance of the Ten Commandments that God the Father gave the world for correct moral conduct'? As a result of these judges' self-imposed liberal views, a distinct disconnection between the Supreme Court, the other federal and state courts and the common sense citizenship is blossoming at an accelerated pace with each morality eliminating decision.

A classic example of liberal judicial contempt toward the citizens of the Republic is the 5th Federal Circuit Court of Appeals' ruling that prayers could occur at graduations but not at athletic events. They stated that graduation was an event "solemn" enough to warrant a prayer, but athletic events were not. Now the judicial system is telling the citizenship they will decide when and where to pray outside of the home or church. What is so great is that many communities are throwing this liberalism back into their collective face.

There is nothing in the Declaration of Independence or the Constitution that gives a judge or a weasel wordsmith the right to change, add, or twist the definition of any word. All English language words and the definition of each are established and accepted by the citizens of the United States as they are documented and printed in all English language dictionaries in the United States. The base foundation for judicial wordsmithing was laid in The Federalist No. 78 paper with Alexander Hamilton's personal interpretation in declaring that the Constitution was defective. This phenomenon created a concept called the "judicial review" starting with Hylton vs. United States in 1796. This "judicial review" concept started the power establishing grab by then Chief Justice John Marshall (a "midnight judge" appointed by the outgoing President John Adams) in an assertive opinion using the case Marbury vs. Madison in 1803 to make the judicial system Supreme Court an equal partner with the Executive and Legislative branches of the federal government. He was able to use this wordsmithing tactic because the Constitution does not in direct wording provide for the power of "judicial review". He used the case to declare the Judiciary Act of 1789 in conflict with Article III, section 2, clause 2 of the Constitution because of its broad wording. This is classical legalese wordsmithing at its best. The "judicial review" is a muddled concept at best.

Because of the above wordsmithing, another major problem developed. It started with the trial lawyers' circuitous path of *using opinions of previous trial case decisions* as if the decision established a law and that future law decisions must conform to previous case interpretations. The trial lawyers use this *prior case law facade* to shuck and jive a decision in their favor. What has become so disturbing about present day administration of justice is that a number of judges have fallen in lock step with the trial lawyers in permitting the *facade of prior case decisions* to establish today's informal laws.

It is too bad that the perception of lost integrity has tainted the legal profession from the top to the bottom because of *injection of prior case decisions* being used in efforts to control and twist verdicts that are not true to the evidence or facts of the case being tried by trying to give the accused the advantage over protection of the victim(s). Wouldn't it be a blessing if common sense returned to rule the day in making decisions and only the facts and true evidence germane to a case would stand as the only items permitted to be offered? This must be one of the Aplomb Society's goals.

Let me inform you of THE NEWEST CASE LAW TWIST being pumped by the trial lawyers' buck and wing soft-shoe vaudeville comedian act. They are now trying to draw in, as being pertinent, trial decisions that are rendered in foreign countries as being a guideline to obtain the decision they want rendered in their trial being conducted in the United States. This scenario was just pulled in a request for a review of a case presented to the Supreme Court where the Court was asked to block a death penalty execution by the lawyer arguing that the penalty would violate international law. He contended that customary international law is law in the United States. You had better watch out for this twist because it will stick you right in your 'ear' when you are not expecting it. Always get this twist eliminated from the trial as soon as it is mentioned. It would not be a small surprise that liberal judges will back flip to get on board over this scheme. There is also a movement going on internationally by loosely connected judicial systems in a few countries to get judges to use other countries' court cases to develop a collage of case law decisions to establish this collage as WORLD LAWS and for all countries to use them as their laws.

The greatest embarrassment to common sense is the perverted logic of the liberal court justice system. Left liberals do not accept the logic of using decent God ordained standards for the betterment of the human race to live by as one family. This is the perversion of wisdom by the indecent exposure of their liberal visionary theorizing of 'anything goes as long as it conforms to a liberal point of view and no one else may have any say as to the liberal rules and you are to just do as you are told' kookaburra doctrine. The voting citizens of the Republic will no longer tolerate this doctrine. I recommend that the citizens laugh in their collective face when they present their liberal arrogance and take them on in the citizens' arena of common sense.

Over time the liberal judicial system will be eroded and will cause the replacement of the liberal hard-core judges with a more logical and common sense thinking group of citizen judges that have the understanding of what the Constitution of the Republic stands for. There are three items you should keep in sight at all times:

(1) When liberal laws or edicts are pronounced, almost always the scopes of some freedoms are compressed.

(2) The citizens must be the final judges as to what law and truth is and make sure that the liberal judicial P-tics are held accountable for their decisions.

(3) Always protect the citizens' right to pass laws when they think the Legislature is not doing their job of protecting the citizenship. Now, out of this come three holistic questions:

> (a) Who decides who needs to be ruled?
>
> (b) Who decides if they want to be ruled?
>
> (c) How is it decided who is to do the ruling?

Could the answer to those questions be—the legal voting citizenship of the United States and not the twisting of arrogate judicial activism?

As I was reading and studying the events leading up to the founding of the Republic and who took the initiative to lead the fight, two questions for community discussion presented itself and they are:

First, 'Why are only people with law degrees sitting as judges'? If you look back in history at who made the decisions of laws and legal documents for mankind, starting with Solomon, David, Moses, all the Founding Fathers, numerous kings, queens and others, you will discover that very, very, very few had any kind of legal or law school background.

That presents the second question, 'why do we need people to hold a law degree to make decisions in a judicative court that require discerning abilities'? Has the law profession become so omnipotent in self-elevation that it perceives itself to be untouchable and they are the only ones qualified to listen, read, write, ask questions, research and render opinions based on facts of the existing problem and not on previous case law from another era?

Test the system in your community and start by running a non-lawyer citizen for a judgeship and see what kind of rules have been set in place to keep the judge/lawyer society in power. If the judical system tries to lock you out with their rules, challenge them with voter-crafted initiatives and with non-liberal oriented jury trials. Start the process!

The *NEXT MAJOR INFRINGEMENT* on the Republic's citizenship is the ILLEGAL ALIEN (illegally trespassing law breaking nonciti-zen), no matter what country they slip in from or conclave they are hiding behind.

People that receive citizenship—by birth or by benevolent Constitutional bequest—must understand that the Republic of the United States is not in existence to be their nanny. As the Constitution so succinctly states, "all men are created equal", not that all people are to stick their hand out, demand a free ride and then ask for more instead of working to support themselves. This sticking out the hand is one principle of the Democratic Party phi-losophy and the citizenship has paid and paid.

A man and woman who are married, the parents of children born out of wedlock, and the single parent are responsible to support the family they created first and foremost. They are not to be required by the P-tics to support *the illegal alien* citizens of another country especially when the legitimate United States citizen is not given a vote as to their opinion. A government that has been created by a legitimate citizenship does not design their Constitution and Bill of Rights to be a welfare country that gives or owes *any illegal aliens* any welfare or any free handouts. The Constitution of the Republic of the United States is designed and states that this country is a Republic and not a liberal mentality democracy.

The responsibility section of the Constitution establishes the job description of the holistic government that mandates: (1) The physical protection by military defense of all citizens, (2) Upholding all legal laws for the protection of the rights of each legal citizen, (3) Giving all citizens the right to find a job, earn a wage to support themselves, and becoming responsible for their personal actions of free choice. *Nowhere* does it say each United States *citizen* or *any out-of-country illegal alien* is entitled to a free handout and then coming back and demanding more as if it is a right. And, *nowhere* does it state that an *illegal alien* has any rights to receive any benefits whatsoever. The question is — why are the *law breaking illegal aliens* receiving any benefits? Why don't they return to their own country, clean up the problems and live in their country of birth? This Republic of the United States started from scratch and was developed by citizens to its present day position who stayed at home working hard with their hands and wiping sweat off their brow. They did not sneak into another country and demand to be taken care of by the citizens of that country as if it is their right to do so. They stayed home and made their own way and earned the right to receive benefits that are needed— because they are ENTITLED to them.

When a legal U.S. citizen is *able to work* and *chooses not to* or *limits* him/herself because he/she does not seek advancement opportunities that are free to everyone as soon as they fill out the applications required and qualify, he/she should not be permitted to receive any benefits. No one should have to hold their hand and lead them to their front door and push them out to go to work. The DECLARATION OF INDEPENDENCE said in the most succinct and comprehendible terms, "We hold these truths to be self-evident, that all men are created equal, that they are endowed by their Creator with certain unalienable Rights, that among these are Life, Liberty and the pursuit of Happiness." NOWHERE does it say in the DECLARATION or the CONSTITUTION or the AMENDMENTS that anyone has the right to demand that the citizenship or any entity support them or owes them any compensation.

If this is the case for the American Citizen, how can any citizen elected P-tic or bureaucrat justify a waver for *any illegal alien* to receive any rights over the United States citizen just *because they broke our laws* and *illegally entered* the United States by sneaking across our borders? It is the responsibility of the *individual illegal alien* and *their parents* to support their family or their extended family members when they need the support. It is their government and the business sector of their country that need to be responsible and responsive to provide jobs. NOWHERE does it state in the Republic's Constitution that *illegal aliens* are to stick out their hands or demand someone else to become responsible for their obligations. The Arizona Senate voted to approve spending $20 million to pay hospitals to provide emergency medical care *for illegal trespassing lawbreaker immigrants* without an approving vote from the Arizona citizenship. The big question is, why doesn't the Arizona Senate bill

President Vicente Fox for the $20 million? The citizenship should demand an answer from the Arizona Senate politicians. This is just another example of P-tic arrogance toward the voting citizenship.

ENOUGH IS ENOUGH CITIZENS; it is time you set this Republic back on the correct path to recovery and start with ridding yourselves of the liberal nonsense you have permitted to be imposed upon you. The American citizen is sitting on their mouth and letting the liberals champion *illegal alien rights* over *citizen rights* and letting the P-tics and bureaucrats of foreign countries dictate the Republic's immigration policies. Call your Community/Townmeetings and develop the start-up agendas to recovery by reestablishing the rights of the citizenship as first priority.

Do you not just get fed up with the constant whining, self-serving criticisms from inept nations of inaction demanding that the United States citizens take care of their responsibilities for their citizens? One of the best ways for these nations to sidestep their responsibilities is by getting rid of their low-income citizens by not trying to improve the working class' living and working conditions. These countries look the other way when someone wants to escape the greed, arrogance and stupidity of their own country. Their governmental P-tics, bureaucrats, the wealthy and business owners take care of themselves first and foremost. Another great burden imposed upon the low-income citizen is the bribery they have to pay to officials just to try to survive.

The Mexican P-tics and others are of the opinion that the United States and the Mexican governments are to share the responsibility for the welfare of the *illegally trespassing Mexican citizen. The big question is what does the word 'share' mean?* The following are examples of two recent Mexican government P-tics arrogate statements directed at the United States. *The first* was by Rosario Green, the previous Foreign Minister of Mexico when he stated " Mexico will use all the political and legal resources at its disposal to guarantee that any violation of the rights and dignity of Mexicans are protected", when Mexican citizens *illegally sneak across* the United States border. He wants the *illegally trespassing lawbreaker noncitizen* to enjoy exactly the same rights as those of a legal American citizen. The great big question is—WHAT RIGHTS? It looks like he is under the misconception that the citizenship of the United States has to comply with any other foreign nation's demands. He has met the wrong United States P-tics; he should come and meet the American citizenship. I am sure they will set him on the correct thinking path.

The second example is the demands by Mexico's President Vicente Fox for the United States to implement legalization for the benefit of *all illegal law breaking undocumented Mexican immigrants* in the United States. Some of his demands that will stick it to the American taxpayer are:

(1) Granting civil rights,

(2) Exemption from visa quotas to legalize migrant flows,

(3) The right of free access,

(4) A guest-worker program,

(5) Receive Social Security cards,

(6) The right to unionize,

(7) College tuition,

(8) Health care,

(9) Driver licenses, and

(10) The option to become United States citizens, to list a few.

He has also stated he will only sign a deal if he gets what he wants. What is so sad for the taxpayer is that the President, the Republican Party and the Democratic Party have jumped on board of this shafting of the American Taxpayer without the vote of the citizenship in any way. And, don't think this is all you will get stuck for. It can easily be increased at any time the P-tic's need more votes from minority groups. Don't you think something ought to be done about this shafting, like immediately?

It is imperative that every citizen e-mail, call, or write and demand from the administration and all members of the House and Senate justification as to why they are handing out jobs to the foreign workers while the American citizenship are getting pink slips. All these two Mexican P-tic's want is for someone else to solve Mexico's problems by saddling United State citizens with their responsibility to provide for the Mexican citizenship that they do not want living in Mexico any longer.

Now that we have seen some of his demands and know that the United States is on top of his hit list, let's take a quick peek at three reasons President Fox wants to promote his agenda to get rid of his poor rural campesinos Mexican citizens:

(1) It has been stated in Mexico that the increased Mexican migration "marked the beginning of La Reconquista, the re-conquering of their lost lands" and refers to the United States as "an old and crumbling empire".

Also, when President Fox made a political visit to Tijuana, Mexico recently he stated that migration "is not a problem. It's an opportunity that we must take advantage of".

(2) A massive demographic shift between the United States and Mexico has created a migration phenomenon for the United States' legal citizenship that will escalate and presents a projected population increase in the United States of Mexican immigrants for the next 75 years.

In the year 2000 there were 34 million Mexicans in the United States. The estimated projections are: (a) by the year 2020 there will be 52 million, (b) by the year 2025—60 million, (c) by 2050—96 million which will represent 47 percent of Mexico's total population living in the United States, and (d) by 2075—142 million.

(3) It is estimated that Mexican immigrants send $7 billion to $10 billion out of the United States to their homes in Mexico each year and the worldwide estimate is $50 billion to $70 billion a year shipped into Mexico. It is unknown how much additional is hand carried into Mexico each year.

With the massive demographic migration from Mexico and the outflow of billions of United States dollars into Mexico each year, Mexico is transitioning into a bedroom nation and the citizenship of the United States is being forced by the United States P-tics and liberals to absorb the burden of supporting the "paisanos" citizenship of Mexico with jobs, medical care, education, etc., etc., etc. This migration is also lifting the responsibilities of President Fox and the Mexican P-tics from having to provide jobs or from developing their country into a viable industrial nation as the United States has done for its citizens. This agenda only leaves Mexico to develop an infrastructure of intrapopulation service outlets to benefit the Mexican government payroll, the business elite, the elite social life, and the mom and pop businesses.

Eleven (11) million have illegally trespassed into the United States by government estimates and it is also estimated that 400,000 more are continuing to sneak across each year. Somewhere the Washington P-tic's have come up with a number of *illegal trespassers* at between 3 million and 4 million Mexicans hiding in the United States. The numbers do not quite work, do they? The presence of millions of *illegal trespassing aliens* is an urgent matter to be rectified with all due speed.

The Congressional Hispanic Caucus demonstrated another example of P-tic arrogance toward the American citizenship when they took it upon themselves to visit with Mexico President Fox and promised to block a Republican proposal in the Senate that tightly restricts *illegal Mexican workers* in the United States. If this Caucus group wanted to be paid lobbyists for Mexico, then they should resign as U. S. Representatives on the citizenship payroll and collect their pay from President Fox.

A prevailing question that must be asked of and answered by *each illegal alien* is "Why did you not stay in your own country and fight to force the P-tics and the power elite to share the benefits they control?" Yes, we have heard all the liberal excuses and nothing is new. What do you think would happen if U.S. citizens pulled a reverse and illegally entered a foreign country in mass? The prisons would be overflowing and no benefits given to anyone. The countries that condone the mass exodus of their citizens, rather than fixing their systems, are looking for internal grievance on a continuing basis established by a foundation of greed, arrogance and stupidity.

Let me give all the soon to be *illegal aliens* and those *already illegally hiding* in the United States something to contemplate and study in depth. There are just two great examples of how to turn a despotic society into shambles. *The first* is the way that Mahatma Gandhi eliminated British rule from India. *The second* is the way the Founding Fathers of the Republic of the United States dismissed the British rule from the United States. These are two effective scenarios with which to reorganize a country. You can rebuild your countries, just as the United States and India had to do. It is strongly recommended that *all want-to-be illegal aliens* and those *"paisanos"* that are *already here illegally* or *legally*, stay in their own country or return home and tell their power elite to share or get ready for a change just as the Mexican citizens in Chiapas have informed them and demonstrated. Stand up like men and be counted instead of running off and hiding. The campesinos have shouldered the Mexican elite arrogates long enough. It is time you returned to you country and make some corrections.

Citizens, it is now time to define the Republic's interest by asking your elected P-tics what makes it too hard and too expensive to shed the *illegal alien* problem? Demand an answer and tell the P-tics to forget the kowtowing. The United States has the means to shut this illegal entry down. I suspect the left liberals and the P-tics feel they know what's best for the citizenship—could that be *illegal alien egalitarianism*? The financial drain of your hard earned money should not be allowed just for the liberals and the P-tics to create programs for *illegally trespassing non-citizens* to live in the United States at your detriment. Could it be they think the *illegal non-citizen* has "more votes and rights" than the citizens of the United States? It is time to play hardball with the P-tics, don't you think? *This illegal situation* will not just disappear until you, the citizen, call a halt to the non-sense and elect common sense citizen legislators to vote for what you, the community, want to happen.

It is now time to start rebuilding a strong single nation, to cross boundaries of class and race and regions through mutual accept-ance and not by attempted force, as is being planned and imple-mented by the self-serving special interest groups. *Take care of the Republic's citizenship first* and then see what the citizens want to do to help other countries—as long as that country first help itself by understanding that the United States' citizenship does not take orders from anyone. The citizenship will decide who gets what. Give the P-tics and bureaucrats notice that they are to ask the cit-izenship what they want to do. Be aware of the fight you will receive from the P-tics and the bureaucrats when they think they have to have your permission to do as they please. Just kick them out of office. That will settle that.

The illegal alien, and present United States P-tics and bureaucrats must stop thinking the Republic is mandated to sacrifice the citizen-ship's time, efforts and resources for their ego, greed for power, and inefficiency. *Think citizens*, you are the only ones who can stop the left liberals, the self-serving P-tics and bureaucrats from taking your hard earned tax money and throwing it down the black hole of leg-islative ignorance. It is time to vote the self-serving P-tic and bureau-crats out of office and give the left liberal mentality the drop kick!

Let us discuss, THE MEDIA. If you look up the definition it says, "something in a middle position". Maybe that is the wrong definition! Would "Gaff Gas" or a "Raree-show" or "the espousing of personal opinions" better fit today's perception of the media? The so-called media of today is overwhelmingly left liberal orientated and biased to the point of amusing stupidity. The left liberal print media and the left liberal radio/television media have deteriorated into nothing more than the mouth of the "lower intestine orifice". They have not only disgraced the news reporting profession and rendered themselves useless by their spewed clichés and sound bits of argot arrogance, but have tainted the honest reporters reputation.

There are *FOUR TYPES OF NEWS OUTLETS* the public has access to: (1) left liberal print media, (2) conservative right print media, (3) the left and right radio/television media, and (4) the in-the-middle media. Lets examine the tenets of how each effects the public through their guardianship of their truth, as they would like the public to believe.

FIRST there are the *LEFT LIBERAL PRINT OUTLETS*, the *CONSERVATIVE RIGHT PRINT OUTLETS* and the greater percentage of the *RADIO/TELEVISION MEDIA*. They all three have the same traits of:

(a) Going to any length to build a consensus,

(b) Being driven by penster verbiage and weasel wordsmiths,

(c) Having paltry clucks, unfortunately,

(d) Engaging in the rhetoric of ridicule imbedded with truth twisting,

(e) Failing to establish truths first,

(f) Overreacting as the norm,

(g) Hungering for the next incident, one that can be dragged out,

(h) Being intolerant of dissent,

(i) Demonstrate that Nihilism has a big play in their mentality,

(j) Trying to rationalize away or dismiss as nothing any subject or statement made that goes against them or when they are caught truth twisting,

(k) Attacking the characteristics of someone to try to discredit them,

(l) Being in the practice of hustling stories before the public as quickly as possible,

(m) Objectivity is not in their playbook, but practicing advocacy is well demonstrated,

(n) Labeling and snickering campaigns,

(o) Watch out when a reporter starts posturing. That is when the reporter starts calling for someone to say something with which he/she can attack a person or create a story with which to take that person down,

(p) When an issue goes against the left liberal media, watch how quickly they become silent and try to hide,

(q) Blathering on subjects they know nothing about, and

(r) Tainting their reporting with personal views by those who essentially are paid to spout off.

These are but a few of the news outlets' common traits. I assume the public has their list.

SECOND there is *IN-THE-MIDDLE MEDIA*. These individual newspersons can be classified as journalists and are rare in numbers. They do not let their personal biases influence the way they cover a story or let the weasel wordsmithing of P-tics, bureaucrats or self-serving special interest groups guide them. They understand the news coverage must be perceived as balanced by diversity, complete, relevant, fair and unbiased and guided by logic, common sense, and reality. If you are lucky enough to locate an *in-the-middle journalist* that has no ego to see their name on a by-line, that understands the definition of common sense truth writing, does not espouse to either side of a viewpoint, and knows how to listen without interruption—this is the person you want placing your issue before the citizenship.

The left liberal media, the right conservative media, and the greater percentage of the radio/television media project their limited thinking abilities by writing and speaking in clichés, sound bits and no substance. It is no wonder the citizenship holds the media in such low regard and having been left to find their punishment in the public indignation. Let it be known that THE APLOMB SOCIETY CITIZENSHIP will no longer tolerate media intolerance of dissent.

What else can be said *about the media* except that the way to eliminate the left liberal media and the conservative right media is to turn the television dial to a station that makes sense *or* cancel the newspaper subscription and challenge them every time they open their parasitic mouth. It is suggested the citizenship only deal with the *IN-THE-MIDDLE MEDIA OUTLETS*.

EMPTINESS

If you want to hide a garbage dump, you enclose it with a facade. The left liberal P-tics, the left liberal individual and the left media have spent the past forty years developing their Potemkin Village garbage dump. The left movement is a mirror image of the Hole-in-the Wall Gang. They would sneak up; attack, and slither back to their hideout until the next attack. This type of attack was well documented in the Florida feeble-minded election fiasco with Gore conceding and recanting and the left medias vacuous integrity. Also, the left liberal drive to undermine or topple the election results demonstrates their monger mentality with no verisimilar in sight. This fiasco validates the great need for extreme urgency to reestablish the Republic under the guidelines of common sense.

Gore and his weasel wordsmiths have not only embarrassed the honest voting Democrats and the rest of the Republic's voting citizenship, he and his gang of weasels drew the voters into his own self interest over that of the American people. They have also provided the world with a chuckle at the immaturity of the schoolyard bullying antics of the Democratic Party by bringing in the Chicago gadflies to do the Democratic Party buck and wing, using the American citizens as a floor for their stage.

Another great media embarrassment was when the left liberal media injected themselves prematurely to become the second real losers not only in the eyes of the common sense citizens of the

United States but also in the eyes of the rest of the world. They will never be able to recover from that stupidity. This election also pointed out that one of the cornerstones for passage to adulthood is the ability to read and write English in the United States and understand instructions printed on paper. Maybe eye examinations, finger weight lifting, and English classes should be mandatory in a few Florida counties.

Another classic Democratic Party left-wing coalition theatrical ploy was the well-planned and orchestrated attack on a United States citizen that was played out on C-Span at the confirmation hearings of Senator John Ashcroft. The liberal left-wing ploy was to neutralize and require Senator Ashcroft to commit his loyalty to the liberal agenda. The left liberal weasels from the Democratic coalition of left-of-center liberal senators and 18 or so liberal groups held a secret meeting in January to develop the strategy to oust John Ashcroft's nomination as U.S. Attorney General. This type of shenanigan is used any time the left-of-center gang becomes terrified of the power someone will inherit, putting the liberal in a subordinate position that they want to control. Another classic example was the hearings of Justice Clarence Thomas for the Supreme Court appointment. This type of political intrigue should be taught in ethics class to demonstrate sleaze of malcontent persons and how liberal campaigns of "sneer and smear" are mounted.

It is time to strip away the façade of left-wing liberalism and eradicate the stench. The following is designed to strip that facade and expose the liberal windmill of arrogance. As it now stands, the majority of the citizenship does not understand how the liberal movement thinks or how it encloses an issue to control the direction they want to go and to achieve the outcome desired. There is also *a truism* that liberals do not grasp, and that is if you start a game with your rules, look over your shoulder for the attack with the *REVERSE RULES*. These rules are set out later in this chapter. These rules will just drive them up a wall, as a liberal cannot understand why anyone would think they are wrong about anything, much less have the gall to attack them.

Let us start stripping away the Potemkin Village facade with a definition of a left liberal and a far right conservative as they are two peas in the same pod: *A megalomaniac despot whose integrity of common sense has been eradicated by the philosophy of self first, nurtured by the process of self-elevating to the omniscient level at any cost to others, thereby establishing their personal and collective agenda as malodorous and putrid.* The left liberals' and the far right conservatives' perceived glories are in their shame, as I have heard someone say.

A peek into the definition above will reveal the left liberal and the far right makeup is fractured nihilism at its worst. Their agendas and causes are gerrymandered in a maze of numerous fellow travelers' philosophies, espoused by the pandering twists of left liberal and right conservative pensters, pundits and weasel wordsmiths. And, because of gaff mentality, the left liberal and far right conservative elements have evolved into an archaic pathetic little joke that lives in the "universe of obsolescence" and are fast achieving the status of persona non grata with the citizenship of common sense.

In the above two paragraphs I have included the far right conservatives to show there are two extremes in politics. The remainder of this chapter will be devoted to the neuroticism of the past forty years of the left liberal elements because of their arrogant personal attacks on others and disregard of the Constitutional rights of legal American citizens. Let's take a tour of the liberal shuck and jive jargon and a few major scenarios as follows.

Let us start by examining *FIVE MAJOR TACTICS* to demonstrate the dark underside of liberalism. To liberals it is a monstrous injustice if they are prevented from doing whatever they wish.

A *first tactic* is to file a notice of intent to sue or try to institute a quick lawsuit splattered with liberal dogma colored by false fear and exaggeration of unsubstantiated rhetoric pretending to be factual for political effect. Then the liberal goes and finds a liberal friendly judge to use and presents a twist of Constitutional wording/law wording intent as a means to achieve their end. But, if they cannot succeed by legalese weasel wordsmithing then they turn to radical patterns of paranoia as illustrated and well documented by the tactics used in the Florida Presidential election. These tactics, orchestrated by the liberals and the Democratic Party in an attempt to overthrow/reverse their loss, would have been laughable had they not represented one of the major political parties and an aspiring presidential candidate of this proud nation. It was a mudslinging, dog and pony show at best.

A *second tactic* used to justify a position a liberal wants to take, even though they have been told no by the citizens or by a court of law, is to commit a tainted act, such as destroying private property, blocking roads, hindering project operations, or other such illegal acts. Then declaring justification of the illegal act as being in the citizens' best interest as the citizens just do not understand the subject. Liberals know that by the result of this maneuver that should any citizen bring suit, the left liberal can try to tie the suit up through the twisting of the liberal justice system and can also have the left liberal media spout their verbal rhetoric stew to make the tainted act out as a correct thing to do or down play an illegal act indicating the citizens and the courts are wrong.

A *third tactic* is to flood a government agency public hearing or a community meeting with conspiracy advocate liberals that live inside and outside the community in order to outnumber the local citizens. A major understanding the citizenship must cement into a mind-set is that liberals will go to any length to build a consensus. Liberals depend on their friendly outside interest groups to show up to help intimidate the local citizens or the staff of the government agencies so they can have their liberal agenda adopted. Liberals also have well rehearsed plans to call upon to disrupt, derail, or control a meeting if the need arises. Liberals will make every attempt to push their agenda and keep the people from hearing or participating in what is being said. I find their disrespect, intolerance of free speech and attempt to suppress opposition by keeping people uninformed tyranny at its lowest level. This liberal scenario is being spread to our smallest communities.

A *fourth tactic* comes into play and is used when a liberal has the pressure applied in an open meeting to present the truth. They resort to *the tactic of discomfit* to try to intimidate an opponent by walking to within three or four feet and facing their antagonist and trying to project a menacing gesture to frustrate, create perplexity and embarrass. Al Gore is the ensign of liberal blackguard cluckism as demonstrated in the debates with his frequent interrupting, exceeding of time limits, speaking out of turn, violating rules, seeking dialogue from the audience, grimacing, chuckling, snorting, and rolling of his eyes. This tactic is a classic example of prime disruptive liberalism at its best. In other words, making fools out of themselves.

A *fifth tactic* is that a liberal will always try to shift a damaging question away from a focus on him/herself by attacking someone else. *Watch the words and phrases* they center upon to draw the attention away from the question being asked by trying to rationalize away or dismiss as nothing any subject or statement made that goes against them or when they are caught twisting the truth. Always keep in mind *the liberal and the P-tic capitalizes his/her answers in clichés and sound bites.* You always know when a liberal is at the bottom of the barrel when they start unleashing the personal insults.

To become more proficient in understanding *the liberal shuck and jive rhetoric stew*, the following few revisionist dilatory verbal clichés and sound bites are prime examples of liberal weasel wordsmithing you will be confronted with or read.

* dismissed the matter as "recycled partisan charges"

* "did not know enough of the facts"

* "no controlling legal authority"

* "no one recalled any particular questions or comments"

* "no evidence he/she heard the statements or understood their implications"

* "drinking a lot of ice tea and may have been in the bathroom"

* "curious, isn't it"

* "would come with a great deal of political liability"

* "environmental extremist"

* "declined to answer"
* "I think...attacked her"
* "extreme-right politics make him a dubious choice"
* "a vast right-wing conspiracy"
* "an ultra-right-wing conservative" (do you think that is the same as a ultra-left-wing liberal flake that goes overboard with their accusations?)
* "lacked the temperament"
* "call the practice heavy-handed and risky"
* "sorta scary" (sort of)
* "the risk here is if we break down this barrier"
* "the benefit to the public outweighs individual privacy concerns"
* "probably"
* a loud, audible sigh, meant to convey profound skepticism
* "trying to scare you with phony numbers"
* "that would threaten the ...."
* "I don't think"
* "serious reservations"
* "try to make guilt by association"
* "try to hide their guilt of association"
* "the facade of trying to talk very solidly and substantially"
* "the charges are laughable"
* "releasing this analysis was not intended to help people make informed choices"

* calling the other side 'conspiracy theorists' when a liberal get caught interfering
* "groundless and partisan vendetta"
* "simply didn't understand"
* "people make mistakes"
* "it's a risky scheme"
* "he was discombobulated"
* "the report was unfair, misleading and rife with innuendo"
* "a political document that buried evidence"
* "he is an unwilling agent and he did not know what was going on"
* "could be"
* "might be"
* "who urged"
* "lets unwrap the package and see what you get"
* "political, unscientific and pushing the envelope"
* "dubva's" or "dubya", referring to President Bush
* "king of low expectations", referring to President Bush
* "will be challenged very publicly"
* "bipartisanship betrayal"
* "forgive and remember"
* "search-and-destroy politics"
* "politics of revenge"
* "filing frivolous lawsuits"
* "I'm not a part of it"

* "very troubled"
* "serious allegations"
* "the ol' Trojan tractor ploy" (?)
* "the people"
* "the people want to know"
* "I speak for all the people when I say"
* "the powerful"
* "too dumb"
* "helmet-haired henchmen"
* "vivacious valets of viciousness"
* "bully boys"
* "ramming"
* "secretly sniggering"
* "blarney"
* "chuckleheaded stuff"
* "civility"
* "tyro"
* "shrinking violet"
* "indicative of a failure of understanding"
* "doltish"
* "the richest 2 percent"
* "paid howlers of the roughhouse right"
* "right-wing howling"
* "the tumbleweed vote"

* "huckstering transparent silliness"
* "putsch"
* "voters were dolts mesmerized"
* "voters were venal"
* "so lame"
* "the cocky, jagged-edged strategist"
* "dark prince of strategy"
* "something surreal"
* "incredibly bad judgment"
* " no evidence of criminal wrong doing"
* "contradicting actions"
* "inflammatory"
* "bigoted"
* "political content"
* "borderline irresponsible"
* "can we afford to take a chance"

These are but a few examples of liberal rhetoric stew and demonstrate the fuel used from their BOVINE LIBERALISM. These verbalizing tactics represent what the left liberal and the left media engage to shuck and jive in order to achieve the stench they want or to play hide and seek with their guilt by pulling out the chips they need.

Now let's look at the *"REVERSE RULES"* of *confrontation* when the left liberal entourage sashays into a meeting or corners you in the hall.

The first "REVERSE RULE" of confrontation is, do not permit any liberal or the media to force you to confront one hostile perception after another. This ploy is one of the oldest scenarios they use to get you rattled so they can latch onto a misquote and write their weasel wordsmith version of the story. Do not even try to confront any charge they make. Just remain silent and go about you business—it will drive them up the wall. Then their last ditch effort will be to make the statement, "The public wants or has the right to know." At this point, turn and look them right in the eyes and ask why they think that, as no one in the public sector has asked you. Then say, "Line up 5 people right this minute who want to know. I am not talking about liberals or reporters, I am talking about 5 qualified common sense citizens and I will talk to them in private."

The *second "REVERSE RULE"* that will come into play is when you attend a hearing or a general public meeting some government agency has called in order to receive public comments on proposed rules, federal, state, and local land grab plans, environmental concerns, or any other subject. The way to participate in any type of government meeting is as follows:

(1) The government agency that called the meeting will explain why the meeting was called and establish an agenda. Ask at this time how the agency will handle interruptions during presentations. If the answer does not meet with your approval, challenge and request a change to benefit all who are in attendance. If the agency bureaucrat refuses to incorporate your request and alter the agenda, ask for his/her name, the address and telephone number of the agency and the name of their immediate boss. Then if the agency does not alter the procedures, decide if you want to attend the meeting or leave. If you stay, lodge

your complaint as outlined in the next paragraph, and then continue as outlined in paragraph 2 below.

Lodge a blistering complaint in writing and by faxes the same or the next day and demand a new meeting with the supervisor or his boss as the department representative. If that does not accomplish your mission, contact your state and federal representatives and the local in-the-middle media. Take the media a copy of all your correspondence sent to the agency and the P-tics and request an article to expose the agency's desire not to cooperate with the citizens.

(2) As the meeting continues the liberals and gadflies will want to take over the meeting. That is just fine. Let them have the floor first to state their position and tell the government bureaucrats what they should do. Then, wait for the agency bureaucrats and any P-tic in attendance to make their statements. You want all the opposition to expose all their plans and verbiage so you will have a clear understanding of what you are up against before you make your presentation.

(3) After item 2 is completed, now is the time to start asking questions and clarifying any weasel wordsmithing that they have injected into their presentation *before* you make your presentation. *Note if* the liberals have told the agency what to do or demanded a delay that is for their benefit. If they have, start by asking the agency representative:

(a) Are the liberals setting the rules for a project, establishing delays, setting deadlines or is the agency still the authority? Get an answer.

(b) Ask pointed questions and demand answers from the liberals and inform them their shuck and jive is no longer accepted. Remember, liberals capitalize their answers in sound bites and clichés. Make them clarify any statement they make.

(c) Ask the P-tics or liberals their reason for a statement, to explain their answers, ask where they live—in or out of the community, who they are affiliated with, how many members do they have, where their financing comes from, what they want and why, and what final goals they want to achieve.

(4) *Now take the floor* and state your case in a well-organized straightforward presentation based on facts, statistics, studies that refute the liberal position, studies that establish your position, petitions and documents that support, and flood the meeting with your supporters. Always use the liberals' own written documents to read out loud and back into their face and always point out the disinformation they are putting out to the public. Do not permit any interruptions from any liberal or P-tic. Tell them they had their chance, so sit down and listen—no cluckism will be allowed. If they continue to interrupt, ask the government bureaucrats to control the meeting or have the ones interrupting removed. If the agency refuses to control the meeting at that point, tell the bureaucrats that their disrespect toward the citizenship has been documented and charges will be filed. This type of scenario is explained in item 1 above. Then decide if you want to stay and fight or walk out en-masse.

(5) If the government does decide to grant a delay for the liberals, do not wait for the agency to 'sort out' the appeal or delay. Tell the judge or agency to stop stalling every time the liberal environmentalists tell/ask them to. If a delay is truly needed, tell the agency the deadline you want and do not take no for an answer. If the agency still capitulates to the liberals, attack the agency's integrity and ask

for the names of the chain of command of that judge/agency and the name of who is handling or blocking the outcome decision. If it does not come out your way, attack them by name and file an appeal (item 1 above) or lawsuit based on what you found out about the liberal strategy.

Tell the left liberal and the left media to abandon their despotism and the fellow traveler philosophy and remember:

(a) in what country they live,

(b) the laws protecting them also protect the citizenship from liberal abuse,

(c) to what country they owe their allegiance,

(d) where they earn a living, and

(e) to observe how the liberal blend of ecstasies affects them every time.

Capitalism has been identified and slandered as a bad thing by the left liberals and the gadfly people who do not miss a meal. What would happen to their stomachs and to their cocktail drinks if capitalism closed all the business doors? What liberal trough would feed them then? Maybe they think the public taxes will provide them with a monthly stipend.

Please do not allow the cowardly terrorist attack of September 11, 2001 that created the solidarity of the political parties and the citizenship give you a sense of feeling that all will change and everyone will have the Republic's best interest at heart. Be alerted that the greed mentality and the self-serving stupidity will start returning even before the first retaliation takes place in response to the attack. The self-serving passive resistance fellow travelers, greedy liberals, power hungry P-tics, gadflies, and the hands out special interest groups will thirst for public exposure by way of their left media print outlets, liberal radio/television provided air time, and the liberals peculiar too-too contrived to-and-fro meandering street dance with which they try to help themselves stay in the limelight. They may even ignorantly help the enemies of the citizenship of the Republic.

The United States P-tics, liberals, and left media are now warned that any and every attempt to continue to pursue their despotism in trying to extend any unwarrantable jurisdiction over the citizens of the United States will be met head-on with the DECLARATION OF INDEPENDENCE, the CONSTITUTION OF THE UNITED STATES, the AMERICAN FLAG, the PLEDGE OF ALLEGIANCE and all they stand for. Their administrative Champion will be THE APLOMB SOCIETY–Citizens Stand Up. Let it be understood by all P-tics, bureaucrats and all on the left—THERE WILL NOT BE ANY MORE ACQUIESCING.

It is time to take a rest from all the stupidity of the liberals, P-tics, and bureaucratic greed we have had to live under for the past forty years. It is time to return to the decision making process that the Founding Fathers set as the example. And remember—"ONE NATION, INDIVISIBLE, WITH LIBERTY AND JUSTICE FOR ALL, UNDER GOD".

PATH

The 1950's came in as a fresh package when the Republic rediscovered the natural phenomenon of having fun in relations with someone or with something tangible. The citizenship had gone through the Korean War-1950/1953 and the diversity of the 1920's interaction of life and the 1940's work ethics were updated with new ideas in the 1950's. Life was fulfilling. Then the left-wing liberal dogma came out from under the outhouse of "psycho-silliness" starting in the 1960's. Life was just too good for the liberals and they started pulling the Republic down with their left-liberal ideas and their stultified street-shows. For the past 40 years, the silent majority and the citizens that sat down on their responsibilities permitted the deterioration to continue. Many logically solid rules and laws were scrambled into fuzzy logic to give the weasel wordsmiths the advantage of instilling the left-liberal doctrine of special interest greed and trying to make liberals the sole guardians of your destiny.

The causes and effects of the downward spiral of loss of integrity suffered by the citizenship of the Republic at the hands of the left-wing liberals and self-serving interest groups has been well covered in the chapters of EXPOSURE and EMPTINESS. This chapter called PATH will give a more clear understanding of other select subjects that are affecting the citizenship. A list of issues that will need to be addressed and reorganized through the Community-meeting/Town-meeting agenda and political warfare will be the focus. Reestablishing the Republic's moral principles and precepts as established by God and put in place by the Founding Fathers will be the primary path and goal to recapture the Republic from the left-wing liberals.

The self-serving liberal greed along with the maze of the liberal ignorant mentalities has created many, many problems over the past 40 years. These problems must be eliminated or revamped to operate efficiently for the benefit of the legal citizenship.

The suggested FIRST ORDER OF BUSINESS is to establish permanent monthly Town-meetings and Community-meetings in every county of the 50 states. How to organize is detailed in the Exposure chapter.

The SECOND ORDER OF DEVELOPMENT is to become aware and come to understand the myriad of issues that confront the daily lives of the citizenship, as we are all confronted with problems on many issues each day. We are continually bombarded by the bombastic rhetoric of P-tics, liberals, the left-wing media news outlets, liberal judges, and left-wing democrats.

The THIRD STEP is to establish a priority list of issues that must be addressed in order of importance.

The FOURTH STEP is to engage with action, demonstrating the sincerity of the community and each individual's commitment to reestablish the Republic for the betterment and happiness of the citizenship.

Before we discuss other selected subjects, let's establish a base list of important topics that confront the citizenship in one form or another almost everyday. The following can be a *start-up list* to be presented at the first Community/Town meeting for the citizens to take home for family and neighborhood discussion groups. The list will also be a good agenda starter at the second Community/Town meeting to break the ice in establishing a priority list of issues to engage that affect a community:

- Term limits (set out in the Exposure chapter)
- Losing your privacy
- Domestic abuse
- Religion vs. government interference
- Reasons for the declining moral values
- Posting the Ten Commandments back on the walls in the school systems
- Faith-based programs
- Racism
- Race-baiting
- Civil rights twisting and slanting
- Reparation for Blacks
- Affirmative action prejudice
- Unethical legal and medical acts public exposure
- Analysis and discussion of Polls (set out in the Exposure chapter)
- Voter-crafted Initiative training class (set out in the Exposure chapter)
- Impeachment and stand for recall training classes

- Illegal Alien problems (set out in the Exposure chapter)
- Liberal Media bias (set out in the Exposure chapter)
- Partial-birth abortion
- Drugs—life imprisonment for dealers and educational programs in schools
- How to help develop a new drug strategy in the War on Drugs (set out in the Path chapter under Drugs)
- Tax reform
- Elimination of taxes and voter approval for any increases in taxes or fees
- Rethink the educational system and curriculums needed for the future (set out in the Path chapter under Education)
- Environmentalist's interference
- Domestic terrorism
- Classes to study The Constitution of the United States
- Hate crimes elimination
- Causes of destruction of family and marriages (set out in the Religion and Family chapter)
- Problems confronted by women, girls and boys in the work place and in education
- Social engineering trends

- Movies and Internet pornography and carnage violence elimination

- Counterattack training to ACLU liberal motives in lawsuits

- The dark side of Banking charges and the ChexSystems database

- Attack on the Boy Scouts' by local, state and federal P-tics, left-liberals and by local school boards and college administrators

- Federal land grabs vs. citizen ownership and recreation rights

- Citizens Health care and Prescription drugs necessity vs. HMO's and Insurance Companies greed and P-tics who take their money and vote to back the desires of the HMO's and Insurance companies

- Drug manufacturers price discrimination policies

- English only as the primary language to be taught in the school systems (set out in the Education section of this chapter))

- Same sex marriage laws

- Pass a law in each state that makes it mandatory that a list be published by the state each month of all doctors and health care companies that have been disciplined or have had a lawsuit filed against them

- Allowing or not allowing judges to collect fees from anyone for outside appearances that could project the connation of improprieties

- P-tics and Government agencies conflict of interest cover-ups

- Overhauling the campaign-finance system

- How to eliminate liberal attack groups full-fledged character assassination techniques of "sneer and smear" campaign rhetoric

- Eliminate commercial advertising in all schools

- Political contributions and corruption

The topics in this chapter are by no means all the subjects the citizenship must address, but these seem to be *the most publicized*. There will be many more topics that will need to be added with new or perhaps more pressing matters, but this is a good-get-started list for now. It is time to call the first Community/Town meeting.

Let's now discuss two additional *PRIORITY SUBJECTS* not covered in the chapters of Exposure and Emptiness as they greatly affect the citizenship as a whole.

The *FIRST SUBJECT* is **EDUCATION** and presents the question— Which should be the educational guardians of the United States, the parents *or* the National Education Association (NEA), the P-tics, bureaucrats, or special interest liberals?

There have been many theories about what is necessary to educate a human because of the diversity of occupations required to sustain the growth and development of a community or a nation. The statement "the nature of society depends on the education of its citizens" is a very solid truism. From the instant a newborn baby smiles back at its Mother—the education for that human has started and will continue until death. From the moment of birth on, the tenets of a proper education is under attack by the points of view of every wind of doctrine dreamed up by man. This wind of mystery has prevailed from the beginning of the human race. But remember, education is not only academic; it also encompasses a myriad of everyday growth variables.

It is unknown at this time when the education mystery will be solved. We all know that the major requirement for employment in the United States marketplace of the business world is the demand for an educated workforce that can fill out an application correctly, be able to speak and read English comprehensible, write English proficiently, spell accurately, and be able to add, subtract, multiply and divide as basic requirements. But, because of liberal theories in experimental education such as social promotions, affirmative action enrollments, and replacement of teaching proper subjects just to focus on the AIMS and SATs tests as the tool to educate the elementary and high school students, experimental education has been a major disaster.

Most of the American school systems have evolved into nothing more than a baby sitter program promoting laziness and second class citizenship steeped in ignorance due to the teaching of the AIMS test answers, replacing the teaching of the total foundation of the basics for education. The underlying goal of the AIMS test is good; however, the test should not be flaunted as teaching the correct education subjects, as the AIMS test teaching is now covering only the selected subject matter that will ultimately be covered by the test. Just to teach the answers to a test by rote is a great mistake. A standardized above minimum level of achievement for each grade level in the United States is a positive requirement and should be enforced. Fortunately, there are a few intelligent parents and offsprings that understand the importance of education and demand it of themselves to achieve at a higher level.

The United States school systems, grades K through 12th grade as they are today, are approaching near obsolescence in the ability to educate for future needed requirements. And, the colleges are right behind and catching up quickly in their inability to educate people for the future. The mentality of teaching has changed little from the start in the first class room to the present day. A great percentage of students become bored, too lazy to learn and disdainful to teachers' authority. Both education systems and their curriculums must be reorganized to achieve a more solid foundation of basic understanding of logic, dialectics, utility, probity, and how to dig for knowledge as soon as possible. The United States has fallen to right above the third world countries in academics. Of the 32 industrialized nations, the American high school student is only ahead of Greece, Italy, Luxembourg, Mexico, and Portugal.

Just for instance, since English is increasingly becoming the world's lingua franca, almost all countries are starting to require their students to learn English as the language of business as a first or second language skill. Our system is lucky if our students can speak, read and write English anywhere near correctly. And, the teaching of basic math problem solving properly has become a lost art in the liberal school systems.

Unfortunately, the experimental education special interest advocators have tried their best to make the United States a multi-language country by trying to have all forms made up in the different languages and, in many schools, English taught as the second language. The United States has been an English-speaking nation from the time the pilgrims landed. The question is, does it not make logical sense that all business forms, correspondence, and government forms be printed in English and English be taught as the primary language in all school systems? All the other culture languages should be taught at home or in school as a foreign language if someone wants to learn one. The ability to speak, read, and write English should be the first prerequisite to owning the right of citizenship.

It is time for the elders of the population, parents, and the community to reclaim their responsibility to oversee the development of education for the secular schools' academic elements and programs being taught to the young children and teenagers of the Republic. The state governments, the federal bureaucracy, P-tics, paid lobbyist, teacher unions, the special agenda interest liberals, the textbook publishers, along with known school administrators and school board members who fall short of the required standard of excellence, must be eliminated from making decisions about education needs. Some of the primary questions, facts and problems about the subject of updating all academic school systems and curriculums are:

(a) Improve progression time for grades K through 12 as it is too long, too slow and promotes students to drop out of school.

(b) Realize that young children have a greater propensity toward retaining information than has been given credence.

(c) Create curriculums that are not rudimentary. Eliminate the studies that create learning boredom.

(d) Require continuing research as to where the voids are in the curriculums being taught to the students.

(e) Teachers should have to spend five years out in the business workforce before they are allowed to teach, but then should be paid commensurately.

(f) Elect a non-aligned school educational system oversight citizens committee to be responsible for evaluating the school boards decisions and evaluate the quality of textbooks to be used by the students.

(g) Make mandatory updating of stronger requirements and curriculums starting at the kindergarten level through the twelfth grade level.

(h) Change class-scheduling times in grade one through grade twelve to the college system of scheduling classes on alternate days and length of class times.

(i) Eliminate college tenure and return all teachers to the classroom full time. Get rid of teachers who do not know how to teach a subject or are too dumb to teach. Political correctness and affirmative action have proven to be a major detriment to progressive education.

(j) Return education to academic integrity and sports to after class participation time with no special perks or treatment permitted.

(k) Add the Olympic minor sports into the school systems. This will give the rest of the 95% student body a chance for a holistic physical education and participation that they have not been offered before. The participants in major school sports are generally the same small group of students and the vast majority of students migrate to spectator status.

(l) Upgrade or replace deteriorating buildings and facilities.

(m) Retain qualified teachers by offering salaries comparable to private industry and incentives to elevate their profession and skills.

(n) Require students to respond with "yes ma'am, no ma'am" and "yes sir, no sir" and stand up when speaking to teachers and adults, with respect.

(o) Establish a uniform dress code to promote cohesion of the student body and to fight against cliques and peer pressure.

(p) Eliminate peer pressure and gang presence, which is hampering student studies.

(q) Reevaluate all textbooks for honest content that states facts and not some person's theory, philosophy or liberal twist doctrine. As an example, the teaching of evolution must be eliminated from being taught as a truth, as there has never been one fact proven as to its existence. Do not permit publishers and salesmen to have any input.

(r) Demand the school board show the teacher's qualifications and abilities to teach, so the parents can give their approval or rejection, before a teacher is hired.

(s) The New Religion of Mother Earth—is your child being indoctrinated in school by liberal teachers teaching them to worship the earth and ignore the constitutional rights of others?

Adults make the assumption that young people have the knowledge to participate in the adult and business worlds just because they have graduated from high school or college. How many of you could not or had great difficulty finding the door knob to open the door to enter the real world. Could it be assumed that you had all the answers and solutions of life until you had to perform in the real world? Remember the ignorance of the peer pressure in high school and college, then in the real world that inundated your life in the first five years after graduation? In hindsight, all the philosophies of immaturity you were confronted with and some people followed, were growth hindrances because the basic foundations to reject them were neither taught nor accepted because of giving into peer pressure, gangs and fads. The participation in and surrender to peer pressure and gang mentality has its establishing roots in a number of negative factors such as:

(1) Lacking of proper parental oversight and follow-ups because of not keeping up with their children's schedules and the kind of friends they run with.

(2) Children not spending time with and learning from Grandmothers, grandfathers, and other mature teachers.

(3) Not attending church or letting God's teaching enter into their lives.

(4) Children being too attached to materialist uselessness.

(5) Not spending quality time with the family.

(6) Substituting family guidance and support for the cowardice of peer group or gang mentality.

(7) Being too lazy to keep a room clean, dressing as if they have no clue, listening to music with a deaf ear, letting the boob tube/video games be the sole entertainment and educational tool, etc.

(8) Showing disrespect toward parents, teachers and the school rules.

(9) Not participating in school programs or sports.

(10)Being too lazy to do homework, letting homework quality slide or being permitted to turn in sloppy homework.

(11) Letting peer pressure, Hollywood programming, advertisements, and the pornographic industry lead children into drinking alcohol, sex, illegal drugs and antisocial behavior.

The ability of a student or child to learn how to control or eliminate self-destructive pressure from controlling or entering into their life requires a combination of coordinated mutual support endeavors such as:

(1) Strong parental participation on a daily bases. Develop the guts to say no to a manipulating whiney self-serving child or teenager. Misbehavior is not to be tolerated at any level as it will lead to the development of major problems. When a child or teenager becomes 'too big for his/her britches', their bad manners can be handled in a number of ways:

(a) Assign psychological chores that require time to complete and that will curtail time needed for desired peer activities.

(b) Take away material items or their allowance.

(c) Sign a contract with them that will be posted in their room each 30 days listing what is not acceptable behavior and the punishment that goes with each offence. Add to the list each 30 days if something new presents itself.

(d) Children are to buy their useless desires with their own money after your approval. But, only after they make a deposit into their checking and savings accounts, which is always set up with a co-signature requirement.

(e) If they have too much time on their hands as they get older, require them to get a part time job.

(f) Require children and teen-agers to dress with dignity at all times for the functions they attend and in public.

(2) School board members' integrity and interest should be to demand:

(a) That the best up-to-date curriculums are taught.

(b) Giving no student an advantage over any other student.

(c) Backing up the responsible teacher.

(d) Getting rid of the incompetent teacher.

(e) School board members and the school district administrators taking the time to visit with the students, parents and teachers on a regular basis.

(f) Establishing zero-tolerance policies for gangs, weapons, teacher disrespect, bullying of students, disruptive students and hazing.

(g) Developing a whole student body yearly calendar with a lot of parent participation.

(h) That parents and school board members demand and help write new juvenile control laws. And, see to it that the state governor and the legislature pass and implement the laws.

(3) The parents, teachers and school board members must demand higher-order thinking from all children and help them by requiring the teaching of mandatory classes in bridge, chess, Greek philosophy logic, problem solving, how money is made, how to save for retirement and other saving requirements, how to understand the stock market and investing, household budgeting and bookkeeping, ballroom dancing, martial arts instruction such as in Tai Chi, penmanship classes, proper grammar and sentence structure classes,

elocution classes, etiquette classes, photography classes with a lab, acting, art classes in paper making-pottery-perspective drawing, the history of the Constitution, how to vote, and hands-on library research, but not internet research. These are some classes that must be integrated into the proper grade levels gradually but started by the second grade. These classes will help develop self-reliance, pride in achieving, self-respect, leadership, and elevation in maturity. Almost all these classes should be taught by true practicing professionals and by developing an alliance with the business community to sponsor teachers from their businesses.

The sorriest excuse of educational leadership has been demonstrated over and over by the nonsense that has been forced upon the children by the P-tic liberals, tax and spend Democrats and liberal moderate Republicans at all levels of government and inept members of school boards. But, the continuing disgrace must be shared between the above and the silent majority and the stand-up citizens who sat down on their responsibilities and permitted logical education to be twisted into a fuzzy mess.

Now to bring your attention to a major trend that has taken root at numerous college campuses that is degrading the educational process. A number of colleges are developing into conclaves for espousing mentally deficient logic of the liberal left idealistic ideas. A true teaching college is supposed to be an academic haven devoted to the teaching of practical necessities, the exchange of ideas and the search for truth. But, the trustees and administrators of these college conclaves are allowing their liberal students to make concentrated efforts in suppressing conservative ideas unpopular to the liberals, which are espoused by sincere students. Failure to project an open arena for learning against those liberal students unwilling to engage in proper debate or not allowing other students and teachers to express an opinion that does not conform to the liberal beliefs, must be eliminated. You should talk to your children and find out what is being taught by their teachers. And, if the child projects a sideways attitude, inform them it is your money that is paying for their aspirations for a college education. If they continue to espouse these troubling ideas ask if they would like to take over the payments. Liberals have become a great threat to academic freedoms of exploration and learning.

To close out this section, I would like to project this idea to the citizenship. The P-tic liberals, tax and spend Democrats, and liberal moderate Republicans must be stopped from defining education by the success of how much money they can spend on useless non-producing programs. And, their partisan desire to keep their constituency under their control, by fighting not to establish correct educational vehicles to improve the chances of children to obtain a quality education, must be brought to the attention of the citizenship each time they pull this stunt. But, be aware that the above groups continuously provide lip service of sincerity of concern as a façade to get you to believe they are working in your best interest. The academic subjects taught must be strong enough to allow students the opportunity to establish their own path to success and get out from under the professional politicians meager and outmoded handouts. The citizenship must eliminate the P-tics, bureaucrats, and special interest parasites from making any rules as to how education programs are to be funded, operated or taught.

The *second subject* is **DRUG'S** and the necessity to obtain a realistic understanding of the complexities of *the drug cartels and the victims who choose to indulge* in the drug culture are paramount. There are many elements attached to the drug culture, all of which are associated with individual mental weakness and greed stimulated by an avarice mentality. This cupidity drive is helping to destroy the character and fabric of the United States and many countries around the world, not to mention the human misery attached to the using of drugs.

The primary funding source for terrorist organizations—whether or not they engage in suppressive control of their own citizens, international terrorism against innocent civilians, or operate in drug cartels—is the money they receive from the selling of their illicit drugs. What is so ironic is that the supporters of terrorism are the self-serving drug heads that purchase the drugs. So the next time you encounter a drug head, ask them who they helped kill today.

What is needed is a factual understanding of the drug world makeup and a detailed insight of its operational procedures to be able to develop efficient elimination programs, toughen the drug laws and run the supports of soft drug laws for the benefit of dealers, pushers and drug users out of town. Let's start by dissecting the drug culture theater of war scenario against the citizens of the world as follows.

To begin, it is critical to agree that the United States' drug policies and liberal drug laws are not severe enough on the cartels' drug lords or the street selling pushers—no matter what age—to stop the flow of drugs into the United States. Until this fiasco can be redesigned by the citizens, not by P-tics and liberal lawyers, to make the selling of drugs inside the boundaries of the United States too severe to be caught selling, none of the existing coddling drug treatment programs will ever work. These coddling programs must be designed for the drug user to eliminate the desire to use drugs or they serve the prison time as a habitual violator. There are also three other parasitical agents that need to be flushed along with the dealers and pushers, and that is the *lawyers* who build their practices solely on defending drug dealers, pushers and users of drugs accused of drug-related crimes; the *lobbyists* who try to buy the vote of weak P-tics to go soft on drug legislation; and the *initiative supporters* who finance procuring initiatives on voting ballots to legalize drugs.

To understand the components attached to the illegal drug culture, you must clearly comprehend THE SUPPLY/DEMAND PATH outlined below. Because of the international criminal organizations operating through highly compartmentalized cell structures, they are hard to pin down. Before a realistic antidrug stance, a strategy, or a policy can be properly developed, you must understand the mechanics of the drug culture as follows.

THE ROOTS AND ROUTES of the supply/demand scenarios start with a collective meeting of a group of criminals set on organizing a family style cartel or, as was the case in Apodaca, Mexico in January 2001, to form an interconnecting national cartel of collaborative drug dealers' "cells". They came together for the purposes of forming a cohesive strategy to protect their greasy little minded business with the following agreements:

(1) "To form a new loosely structured cartel that would unite their operations and cut their individual overhead";

(2) To devise a joint strategy for selling drugs within Mexico and exporting drugs into the United States;

(3) They also "Agreed to end their infighting"; and

(4) The drug dealers "Agreed to increase the violence in an effort to destabilize the Mexican government."

This meeting was called because they were stepping on each other too much and because the United States law enforcement interception endeavors are putting a real clamp on the illegal drug traffic deliveries.

The second link in the supply/demand path is to *PLANT* and *HARVEST* the illicit base coca, opium, marijuana, potent marijuana, and Indian hemp crops in many divers locations to try to keep from being detected by the drug eradication forces. This link and their success can only be accomplished by exploiting weaknesses and paying off the corrupt politically connected P-tics, the judicial systems, government officials, the military and police personnel, all who have sold themselves into the drug culture. Drug corruption penetrates all levels of governments and become entrenched at the local levels because of the need of the campesinos and the populations of the outlying towns or villages to support their families and because of this need they end up becoming captive laborers.

The *third link* is the *MANUFACTURING* of the raw materials into a usable product and the packaging of the merchandise for shipping to the wholesalers. There are two types of manufacturing techniques used: (1) the processing of raw plant related materials listed above; and (2) the skilled and unskilled drug chemist who develops the hybrid drug chemical compounds as follows.

The *hybrid drugs* are developed in what is called Clandestine Labs. These labs are illicit operations that employ some operators who have little or no training in chemistry and follow underground recipes. But, some of the labs employ chemistry students or professionals as processors.

The following is a PRIMARY LIST OF HYBRID SYNTHETIC DRUGS that are very dangerous toxic substances known collectively as designer "CLUB DRUGS" and are increasing in popularity. They will produce long-term damage to the brain and death in many cases. Many of the drug-use trends are still emerging. There are also other hybrid drugs that show up from time-to-time and disappear for whatever the reason.

(1) MDMA(Ecstasy)—(3,4-Methylenedioxymethamphetamine) is a Schedule 1 synthetic, psychoactive drug with both stimulant (amphetamine-like) and hallucinogenic (LSD-like) properties that are also neurotoxic. Chemically, it is an analogue of MDA. Its effects last approximately 4 to 6 hours. The user may be at risk of permanent brain damage. The street names for this junk are Ecstasy, XTC, X, Adam, Clarity, Lover's Speed, hug, beans, and love drug.

(2) PMA(Paramethoxyamphetamine)—is a methoxylated phenethylamine derivative that is sold under the semblance of "ecstasy". It is a fake Ecstasy, called PMA and PMMA. If someone takes these pills, there is a chance they will die because it will raise the body temperature to as high as 108 degrees. The street names for this killer are Death, Chicken Yellow, and Chicken Powder.

(3) GHB(Gamma-hydroxybutyrate)—is a central nervous system depressant that can relax or sedate the body. It is used for its intoxicating/sedative/euphoriant properties and for its growth

hormone-releasing effects. This drug has been increasingly involved in poisonings, overdoses, "date rapes", and death. Its effects begin 10 to 20 minutes after the drug has been taken and can last up to 4 hours. The street names are Liquid Ecstasy, G, Grievous Bodily Harm, and Georgia Home Boy.

(4) Ketamine—is an injectable anesthetic and is produced in liquid form or as a white powder that can produce hallucinations and dream-like states. It is often used with marijuana or a tobacco product. The street names are K, Cat Valiums, Special K, and Vitamin K.

(5) Rohypnol®(Flunitrazepam)—is a benzodiazepine that is a tasteless and odorless drug that has a sedative and toxic effect that is aggravated by use of alcohol. The drug's effects begin within 30 minutes, peak within 2 hours and can impair a victim for 8 to 12 hours. Withdrawal seizures can occur a week or more after cessation of use. It can cause profound "anterograde amnesia" causing a person not to remember events they have experienced. The street names are Forget-me Pill, Rophies, Roofies, Roche, Rophy, Mexican valium, Rib, Roach-2, Rope, Ropies, R-2, and Roaches.

(6) Metamphetamine—is a neurotoxic, addictive stimulant that affects the central nervous system. It is a white, odorless, bitter-trasting crystalline powder. It can cause memory loss, aggression, violence, psychotic behavior, cardiac and neurological damage, and the transmission of infectious diseases. The street names are Glass, Chalk, and Speed. Fire, Ice, Meth, and Crystal.

(7) LSD(Lysergic Acid Diethlamide)—is a hallucinogenic substance produced by an organic compound that has two long-term disorders associated with it—persistent psychosis and hallucinogen

persisting perception disorder(flashbacks). The street names are Yellow Sunshines, Acid, and Boomers.

(8) Crack—is a highly purified cocaine especially potent and addicting that will lead the user into a biological counterpart of hell that will prolong suffering beyond the bounds of normal human experience and death. The street name is Rock.

The *fourth link* is the *WHOLESALER* who can be the drug product owner or a middleman representing the owner. When someone wants to purchase illicit drugs, a meeting between the seller and buyer is set up. This meeting is started with everyone trying to establish his or her machismo. After this exercise of schoolyard bulling, the meeting takes place. At this meeting a number of details are settled, such as the quantity of drugs needed, the quality of the drugs wanted, negotiation on the price, how the purchase money payment and the exchange of the money and drugs will be handled, the delivery location, and the date of delivery is arranged. Then the drugs move along the path to the next link in the operation.

The *fifth link* is the in-country *TRANSPORTATION* of the illicit drugs from the growers warehouse to the out-of-country smugglers network warehouses. The trafficking in illicit drugs is controlled by the international organized drug cartels and they model their operations after terrorist tactics for safety and security. The safe transportation of the illicit drugs is the responsibility of the owner/seller until the drugs are delivered to the buyer, whether in or out of the country.

The *sixth link* is the *SMUGGLING* of the illicit drugs to the distribution points. If the target country is the United States, the illicit

drugs are smuggled in and delivered to one or more distribution outlets to be paid for and to be distributed by the United States whole-
sale illicit drug dealer to the original drug buyer or sold to drug
dealers selling at the street "retail" level. There are three major vio-
lent types of gangs involved in the street sales of the illicit drugs: (1)
traditional street gangs, (2) outlaw motorcycle gangs, and (3) prison
gangs. Now, the drugs move into the drug culture world to be sold.

To give you a few examples of some amounts of drugs the criminal smugglers have been caught trying to smuggle into the United
States: (1) On May 3, 2001 the Coast Guard made the biggest
cocaine seizure in United States maritime history. They seized 13
tons with a street value of around $500 million dollars. The previous
record was 12 tons in 1995; (2) In fiscal year 2000, about 60 tons
total was seized; (3) In North Carolina 4 tons of Mexican marijuana
and $1.4 million dollars in cash were seized at a farm. (4) On
October 3, 2001 the Customs official in Blaine, Washington seized
980 pounds of potent marijuana called "B.C. bud" worth around $8
million dollars. (5) On November 14, 2001 the Mexican Navy
found 1.5 tons of cocaine buried on a beach in the state of Oaxaca.
The Union of Myanmar authorities destroyed nearly $1 billion dol-
lars worth of amphetamines, opium and heroin recently in their
efforts to stop its illicit drug trade.

This is just a chip off the iceberg of the amounts delivered into
the United States each year. It is estimated that the international
illicit drug business generates as much as $400 billion dollars or
more in trade each year around the world. Staggering, isn't it?

The *final link* is the demand side of the supply/demand path.
That is the *INDIVIDUAL CONSUMPTION BUYER* (the Idiots).

The drug using idiots are two-thirds of the out-of-control drug problem around the world. The remaining one-third of the problem is the liberal drug laws, drug defense lawyers, lily-livered liberal judges, the nitwit liberal jurors, and the supporters of "let us do what we want" drug initiatives that want to sanction illegal illicit drug use. Not only are the supporters of the drug culture opposed to the drug war being fought by the Unite States and local governments, they truly want to eliminate all opposition.

To give you ballpark figures of some *estimated purchases* and some of the amounts of *your tax money being wasted* in fighting the war against drugs as now being fought, purchasing drugs, and cost of drug treatment programs, observe the following:

(A) It is estimated that $65 billion dollars are spent each year to purchase illicit drugs in the United States.

(B) An estimated 15 million plus Americans used illicit drugs in 1999 alone.

(C) It is estimated that in the year 2000, the federal, state, and local governments combined, spent $31 billion dollars to combat the illicit drug market.

(D) The federal anti-drug budget in the year 2000 was around $20 billion alone.

(E) In the next 5-1/2 years, California has budgeted $600 million to place self-serving drug offenders in community treatment programs.

(F) An already approved anti-drug gift package of $1.3 billion dollars will be given to Colombia for a show and tell drug program. Now the Colombian P-tics want an additional $600 million more of the American citizens' tax dollars to spend. This does not include the enforcement personnel instructors sent in to help train their enforcement troops. Wouldn't it be of interest to see who gets fat from this fiasco!

(G) It used-to-be assumed the drug and gang problems were a product of the inner cities. The wake up call has arrived with the discovery that the drug culture and the gang cowards have arrived in utopia and have now become a rural and suburban problem at an alarming rate.

(H) It is estimated that around 20,000 humans die from illicit drugs each year around the world.

This is just a blush of a glance of the total waste of your tax paid dollars spent on government programs and the coddling of self-serving drug users by the P-tics that disregard their sworn obligation to protect your tax dollars for the benefit of the Citizenship. It is now time for the Citizenship to kick the tax and spend P-tics and bureaucrats out of office for the benefit of the United States citizens and the non-citizens around the world. Let's face reality, if they are not replaced with the logical thinking Citizens, *along with voting into law a very, very hard drug policy* and *very hard punishment laws to back up the drug policy*, the citizenship will have failed to take back the garden that God gave to us to live in and will witness the destruction of the Republic's future and the future of families for the self-serving benefit of the P-tic power grabber and free basing drug addict.

The only one who can decide what is important is the individual citizen. You are the only one that will have to answer to your children when they ask—why did you think someone else was more important! Which leads to the "If" word, and that is the big "IF". IF the United States citizenship would eliminate *all* the waste of tax money spent by and on *all* the Untied States P-tics and bureaucratic non-sense programs and applied *all* that money to re-structuring the infrastructure of the United States. Imagine how this re-capturing of wasted money would help the Republic turn around!

Take a very hard look around and come to the realization that—it is now time to call the Citizenship communities together and set the agendas to take this Republic back from the self-serving evil trying to destroy you, your family and this great Republic!!

Who should spend all the billions, the idiots, United States P-tics, bureaucrats' or the legal United State Citizenship? Your choice.

RELIGION AND FAMILY

In this closing chapter I would like to draw the Citizenship's attention to the paramount elements that will help reestablish the base foundation in returning the Republic to the path of greatness. That foundation is the acceptance of God as the Supreme Father and three of His most spiritual and precious gifts that He has given to His children on earth. These are His Ten Commandments, Ordinances, and Statutes that teaches morality and correct interaction with others by setting forth guidance to parents of subjects to be taught to the children, guidance for the children to understand their responsibilities for respecting their parents and for them to learn self-respect as required in becoming responsible future adults and parents.

Religion and the single parent or the two-parent families are as interwoven as the Dodder vine, also called the "love vine". It is a known fact that parents and their children mature into a holistic family relationship faster when they attend church, explore life, study and play together on a consistent loving path into the maze of parenthood as the children grow into adulthood. The idiocy of ignorant parenting must be stopped and the community must insist upon correct behavior in public from the parent/child interaction and singly. The ignorant parent/disrespectful child interaction inside a home has to be corrected by law or other remedies inserted, starting with ethical Christian counsellorship.

There are a number of foundation building blocks that lead to a successful marriage and a functional multidirectional family relationship. The foundation block that opens the path to a successful respect of others is the building block called "proper Courtship". The word "courtship" is divided into two properties: premarital of the formative years and postnuptial. It all starts with demonstrating proper husband and wife relationships and the teaching of God's teachings to the children when they are at the young age of observance, acceptability, mimicking, mind storage, motivation to help, starting the process of understanding the balancing of good and bad actions, and the beginning of regulating their minds.

The teaching of "proper courtship" accomplishes two very essential elements. *One* is it establishes an ethical foundation for a child to use to guide them through the nitwit mentality of peer pressure and the ability to reject the sleazy trash music, Tinseltown's useless garbage and the internet pornographic filth. The *second element* is for the Mother's, Father's and past lost loves to reinvigorate the enthusiasm of the first youthful realization of wanting to be together and the opportunity to reintroduce courtship back into their daily lives. The "I Do" does not stop the path of courtship; it just moves the excitement to a higher plane.

Mothers and Fathers, make it your responsibility to resurrect the culture of the courtship tradition of respect and fun with others in growing and discovering together. Children want strong family ties and know that it is of utmost importance for their success in learning and achieving goals. Children will observe on a daily basis if mother and father are living up to the rules they teach and will observe each infraction and the good points of their parents' everyday courtship toward each other.

This interaction between husband and wife will let them see first hand the beauty of a good marriage relationship and parental cohesion. Believe it or not, children do think and keenly observe.

There are two major causes for the deterioration of a lasting marriage. *The first major loss* to a long lasting marriage is the loss of understanding of the rules of daily courtship. Courtship is the path to discovery of the positive and negative traits for evaluation through the maturation of opposing sexes. The abdication of courtship started in the 1960's with the dropout flower children from the maturity required to become responsible adults and leaders and in helping to keep the sanctity of marriage as the foundation of the principles, values and virtues that contributed to establishing the United States. As a result of the flower children's liberal mentality, it is evident that the internal destruction of the family has taken its toll on the quality of many children in today's society because of adult capitulation to self-serving children.

The second major cause for the loss of the courtship tradition has been the number of liberal sociopathic man-made discrimination ideologies that have turned God's beautiful gifts into a framework that has perverted courtship as a correct path to marriage and replaced it with liberal prattle of just live together, liberal self-serving drug culture and anything goes as long as it is liberal. All of these things lead to marriage breakdown or less-successful marriages. One of the liberal movement's main objectives is to eradicate Christianity so that they will not be held accountable for their actions in their own minds and will be able to write their own laws and behavioral doctrine of depravity. This perversion has allowed them to bow down to worship their materiel/stultified gods as seen through their minds eye for justification to do as they please. It is time to kick this idiot mentality out the back door of life.

There are *two separate elements* in the tradition of courtship. *The first* is precourtship—before marriage maturation and *second*, postcourtship—after marriage interdependence. Also, there are cultural traditions in each subculture that are too diversified and out of the scope of this presentation. But, there are basic courtship rules and understandings of any culture that establish the teaching paths that Mothers and Fathers must instill in the permanent psyche of a mind-maturing child. The precourtship phase is the very best time to entrench lasting ethics and eliminate the liberal ideological bile that confronts maturing children. The following are *three understandings* and *nine suggestions* for the beginning of courtship training and family growth process:

(a) There are male charmers and female receivers of attention.

(b) Mothers set the children's household and in public behavioral rules that they are to follow. She is the ethics and homework monitor and is in-charge of the household management programs. Mothers, do not forget to teach your daughters about the female instinct.

(c) Fathers are the children's primary outdoor activities, outdoor chores, and the street-wise survival teacher. He is the back up disciplinarian for the Mother.

(d) Establish a night of the week to sit down as a family to study scripture, talk about family business and personal problems that a child needs help to resolve. It would also be good if the parents put out for discussion some of their problems and would ask the children if they have a suggestion for a solution. This will give the children the feeling of belonging and teach them how to interact with family members and realize other family members also have problems. This will also teach them how the analysis and decision process works in a group setting. Be sure to make this a fun time for all participates.

(e) Boys and girls are to be taught not to pressure someone to do something they do not want to do. This is another type of bullying and should be stressed as being a bad trait.

(f) Children must be taught the rules of correct behavior. Do not permit them to skip past any behavioral rules, in or out of the home. Manners taught at home will be carried into adulthood.

(g) Teach the children the basics of cooking and help them to grow into young chefs. Also, teach them to prepare and host sit down dinners and throw barbecues for their friends. This is a great way to develop social skills, table etiquette and self-confidence. It also helps them not to starve when they move out. Don't forget to teach them how to do laundry and basic household chores also.

(h) Boys must be taught by both parents to respect the female when she says no and the girl must be taught to respect the boy when he says he does not want to do something.

(i) An interwoven theme that sex must wait until the night of the marriage vows must be entrenched from the first day of their capacity to understand. Smoking, using drugs and drinking must also be taught as not acceptable. And, hopefully all that will carry on throughout their lifetime.

(j) The rules of virginity must be instilled in both the boy and girl by both parents through their sex education path to adulthood and into marriage. Once they understand the importance of the rules, hopefully the young people will respect themselves enough to adhere to the rules and pass the rules on to their children.

(k) Mothers should teach the boys how to properly invite a young lady to a function, how to go to the door to pick her up, meet the parents and return her to the door, intact.

(l) Parents should not allow a child to belong to a gang or a clique of any form.

Just as the Mother and Father are the glue that holds the family together, the family and the Constitution are the glue that holds the Republic together. But, God is the one who holds our destiny and the Republic's future in his hands. We as a holistic nation must come back to that realization if the family and the nation are going to stay in business. The liberals and the Supreme Court have told God that his teachings don't count. This was not very smart and they will have to account for their rejections. Woodrow Wilson said: "America was born a Christian nation. America was born to exemplify that devotion to the elements of righteousness…are derived from the revelation of the Holy Scripture." Family scriptural group study, prayer and family attendance at church is by far the best foundation a family and an individual could have to develop their trusting link to God, to understand what the privilege of citizenship represents, and to realize their responsibilities toward each family member and to their true friends.

As I close this book, I would like to leave this thought with the Citizenship— it is in your hands to turn this great nation around and reestablishing the understanding of being proud we are Americans that live in a free choice and individual freedom country.

Have a great future, VOTE FOR AND LIVE THE CHANGE.

0-595-21582-3

www.ingramcontent.com/pod-product-compliance
Lightning Source LLC
Chambersburg PA
CBHW031233280526
45784CB00004B/1557